D0349559

THE GARDEN BIRD BOOK

First published in 2007 by New Holland Publishers
London • Cape Town • Sydney • Auckland
www.newhollandpublishers.com

Garfield House, 86–88 Edgware Road, London, W2 2EA, United Kingdom
80 McKenzie Street, Cape Town, 8001, South Africa
14 Aquatic Drive, Frenchs Forest, NSW 2086, Australia
218 Lake Road, Northcote, Auckland, New Zealand

Copyright © 2007 in text: Sarah Whittley
Copyright © 2007 in artwork: New Holland Publishers (UK) Ltd
Copyright © 2007 New Holland Publishers (UK) Ltd including the year of first
publication

10 9 8 7 6 5 4 3 2 1

All rights reserved. No part of this publication may be reproduced, stored in
a retrieval system or transmitted, in any form or by any means, electronic,
mechanical, photocopying, recording or otherwise, without the prior written
permission of the publishers and the copyright holders.

ISBN 978 1 84537 496 9

Although the publishers have made every effort to ensure that information
contained in this book was meticulously researched and correct at the time of
going to press, they accept no responsibility for any inaccuracies, loss, injury
or inconvenience sustained by any person using this book as reference.

Editorial Director: Jo Hemmings
Senior Editor: James Parry
Cover Design & Concept Designer: Adam Morris
Designer: Gülen Shevki-Taylor
Production: Joan Woodroffe

Reproduction by Modern Age Repro Co, Hong K
Printed and bound in Malaysia by Times Offset (

KENT LIBRARIES AND ARCHIVES	
C 153034493	
Askews	

THE
GARDEN
BIRD
BOOK

Text by Sarah Whittley
Illustrations by Dan Cole

NEW HOLLAND

Contents

MORE UNUSUAL GARDEN VISITORS IN BRITAIN AND EUROPE

Further Reading and Useful Addresses

Birds in Gardens

Birds are part of our everyday lives, and never more so than when we see them in our gardens. Whether located deep in the heart of a bustling city or out in the relative peace of the open countryside, there can be very few gardens that never receive a visit from a bird. For many millions of people, garden birds provide a year-round source of interest and enjoyment, with considerable amounts of human time, money and energy spent feeding them and providing the conditions in which they will hopefully thrive. Although gardens have been an important refuge for birds for hundreds of years, recent decades have seen their value to birds in Europe, and particularly in Britain, grow in signficance to the extent that they now constitute a major habitat for a wide variety of bird species, many of which are woodland inhabitants that have made the transition to suburban and urban life. With so many people putting out bird food and planting wildlife-friendly gardens, the future for garden birds has perhaps never looked so bright.

Bird Topography

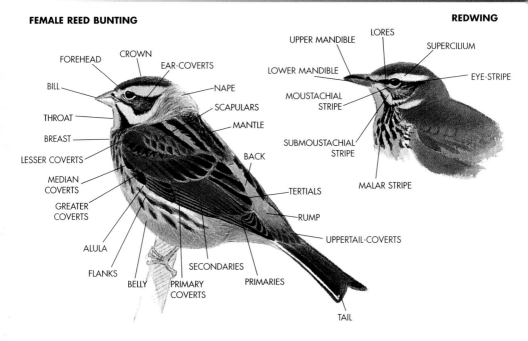

FEMALE REED BUNTING

FOREHEAD
CROWN
EAR-COVERTS
BILL
NAPE
SCAPULARS
THROAT
MANTLE
BREAST
LESSER COVERTS
BACK
MEDIAN COVERTS
GREATER COVERTS
TERTIALS
ALULA
RUMP
FLANKS
SECONDARIES
BELLY
PRIMARY COVERTS
PRIMARIES

REDWING

LORES
UPPER MANDIBLE
SUPERCILIUM
LOWER MANDIBLE
EYE-STRIPE
MOUSTACHIAL STRIPE
SUBMOUSTACHIAL STRIPE
MALAR STRIPE

About the British Trust for Ornithology

The British Trust for Ornithology (BTO) is a unique partnership of volunteer birders and scientists, dedicated to understanding more about the United Kingdom's birds and the reasons for changes in their populations and distributions. By using a combination of surveys and other techniques such as ringing, the BTO has been able to alert the public, government and policy-makers about the plight of many of our bird species, including those occurring regularly in gardens.

People involved with the BTO and its surveys range from experienced birders taking part in specialized survey work to the thousands of people that watch birds in their gardens and contribute to the BTO/CJ Garden BirdWatch Survey. This survey, and others like it, continue to reveal valuable information about trends in garden bird populations and can even help explain the reasons behind the recent decline in numbers of species such as Song Thrush and Spotted Flycatcher.

For more information on how to take part in garden bird surveys, please contact GBW, BTO, The Nunnery, Thetford, Norfolk, IP24 2PU or email: gbw@bto.org. Further details on the work of the BTO generally is available from the same address and also at www.bto.org.

How Likely Am I To See....?

The data collated for the BTO/CJ Garden BirdWatch Survey has been used to give an indication in this book of how regularly individual species are recorded in British gardens. A 'garden ranking' is given in each case, as follows:

- VERY COMMON: Recorded in over 75 per cent of gardens surveyed in a ten-year period
- COMMON: Recorded in 50–74 per cent of gardens
- LESS COMMON: Recorded in 25–49 per cent of gardens
- UNCOMMON: Recorded in 10–24 per cent of gardens
- RARE: Recorded in up to 9 per cent of gardens

Of course, it is impossible to give anything other than a general indication of how likely a particular species is to appear in your own garden; much will depend on where in the country you live, how big your garden is and what sort of habitats it contains. Further information about these site-specific factors is given in each species account.

Attracting birds to your garden

A GUIDE TO BIRD FOOD

With roughly half the human population of Britain feeding their garden birds, there are many different bird foods on the market. Knowing just what to buy for which species of bird can be a bit of a minefield, so below is a list of typical bird food available from high-street shops. If you're lucky enough to have a local farmer who grows birdseed crops, you'll find the prices far cheaper; if not, any reputable brand will suffice. On the whole, most seed mixes are fine, but beware: some of the less reputable mixes use dog biscuits (small pink or yellow lumps) to add bulk. These biscuits can cause harm by swelling up in the stomach. Other mixes use grain, which is only of use if you want to feed pigeons, doves or pheasants.

What do Birds Need?

Birds need feeding for several reasons: to stay alive during severe winter weather; to get through periods when their natural food may be in short supply; to be in good condition for the breeding season; and to feed their young. This means feeding birds throughout the year, something the BTO has advocated for many years. In late autumn and winter months, foods with a high-fat content really help: fatballs, peanuts and cheese, for example. During spring and summer, birds need to feed their young high-protein food, such as mealworms. Specialist food such as oyster-shell grit, which is rich in calcium, can be important during the breeding season. Drinking water is often overlooked, but it is vital for bird survival, especially during winter when standing water is frozen, and in high summer when water can disappear altogether.

Grains and Seeds

- Black sunflower seeds are a great year-round food. They are very nutritious and have a higher oil content than the striped ones. Tits and finches love them.
- Sunflower hearts have the black outer husk already removed, thus enabling quick access to high calorific food without the messy husks discarded under the table.

- Nyjer seeds come from an Ethiopian plant called ramtil. The tiny, black seeds are high in rich oils and are a particular favourite with Goldfinches, Redpolls and Siskins.
- Hemp seeds are great for tits and Nuthatches; it is a pleasure to watch them try to crack the seeds open with their bills.
- Millet seeds have a high starch content and are full of essential minerals, amino acids and vitamins. House Sparrows, Dunnocks, finches, Reed Buntings and Collared Doves favour this food.
- Wheat and barley grains contain vitamins, minerals and carbohydrates, and are suitable for birds like sparrows, pigeons, doves and pheasants.
- Rolled oats are a great, relatively cheap protein-rich food. It is best to buy the rolled variety, as birds find it tricky removing the tough outer husk.

Peanuts

These are probably the most popular garden bird food available, and are suitable for a variety of birds, such as tits, woodpeckers, Jays and sparrows. But beware - always buy a known brand that has been tested to ensure freedom from aflatoxin, a naturally occurring toxin that can kill birds. Reputable companies either belong to the Birdcare Standards Association or test to the appropriate standards.

Peanut logs are easy to make, and are a great way to encourage otherwise shy birds into the garden. You can buy a ready-made log with holes, or you can drill out your own, then fill them with peanut butter – crunchy is best, especially if it's organic! Mix in other nuts and seeds to make an even better feast. The sort of birds you'll be attracting with this feeder are Nuthatches, woodpeckers and Treecreepers, although many more will be intrigued. Other nuts such as hazelnuts, almonds and walnuts are all good food for birds. However, never feed salted nuts to birds, as these can be lethal.

Fatballs and Suet

Although it's easy to buy various fat-based bird-feeding products, from fatballs to cakes and blocks, it's also very straightforward to make your own. Melted lard, suet and a mixture of seeds, cheese and peanuts mixed in a bowl then left to set is an effective and economical way to feed birds. You can use old plastic food containers, mugs, or silver trays to put the food in. Putting string in the wet mix allows you to hang up your own feeders, too. Shredded suet is a good winter food because of its high fat and calorie count. Albeit rarely, the fine, plastic mesh surrounding bought fatballs has been known to trap birds' feet and tongues. If you are concerned by this potential low risk, then remove the mesh bag and dispense the balls from an appropriate feeder.

Insect foods

With all the different seed foods on the market, it is easy to overlook insectivorous birds, which would be a mistake, as most species feed their nestlings on insects. Nowadays, pet stores and bird-food suppliers sell a variety of food, including mealworms, waxworms and ant pupae. This food attracts Robins, wagtails and Starlings.

10

Fresh Fruit

Fruit is enjoyed by a variety of birds, especially Blackbirds, thrushes and Starlings. Apples, pears, bananas and grapes, either hung up or scattered on the ground, will attract these birds. If you are putting out the fruit during the winter months, make sure you clear away any snow that has fallen. Hanging fruit from trees can prevent the snow from hiding the food. Remember to cut up any fruit, as smaller pieces will help the birds to get to the food more quickly.

Dried Fruit

Raisins, sultanas, currants and apricots are excellent dried fruits for birds, but they are best soaked overnight during the spring and summer months, to ensure nestlings don't choke. Any larger dried fruits should be finely chopped. Dried fruit is a particular favourite of Blackbirds, Song Thrushes and Robins.

Household scraps

Many kitchen scraps are suitable for birds, but make sure that everything you put out is cut up into tiny pieces so that the birds don't choke. Pastry, either cooked or uncooked, is a good fatty food. Potatoes, either baked, roasted or mashed with seeds, are popular. High in fat, cheese is a favourite of Robins, Blackbirds, thrushes and Dunnocks; even Wrens will be tempted when it's grated finely. It is okay to feed bread to birds, but brown is better, as white can have little nutritional value (unless nutrients have been added to it). Make sure the bread is in small crumbs, so it doesn't swell up in the birds' stomachs. Cooked rice and pasta is a good food as it is full of starch, but make sure that it isn't cooked with salt, as too much salt can kill birds.

Meat can be a real hit with some birds, and many households put out bacon rind and animal fat on the bird-table (salty bacon and smoked bacon are bad for birds, however). Cat food (meat, not biscuits) is very popular with a variety of birds, Blackbirds especially. Sometimes, the birds will bring their hungry fledglings to cat bowls, gorging until all the food is gone. Hanging a bone or carcass on a piece of string can attract woodpeckers, crows, tits and Starlings.

THE BEST BIRD-TABLES AND FEEDERS

Buying a bird-table was once a simple task; they consisted of a straightforward wooden hut on a long pole, with hooks from which to hang feeders. How things have changed! The product range is now so huge and varied that you need a whole afternoon to decide which one is right for you. To be honest, the old fashioned bird-tables are still just as good.

Buying a Bird-table

There are a few questions you should ask:

- *Do I need a standing or hanging bird-table?*
  The latter is good if space is limited, or if there are lots of cats around.

- *Should I have a high roof, low roof or no roof?*
  High roofs allow good viewing and access for larger birds. Low roofs stop larger birds such as pigeons, but viewing is more limited. No roof is great for viewing, but rain can make food soggy. Never buy a bird-table that has a nestbox incorporated into its roof.
  Look for a rim around the sides to stop food from falling off. A gap in the rim is essential to aid cleaning and to help water drain away. A hole at each corner of the base also helps with drainage.

Buying a Bird-feeder

The multitude of feeder types, designs and sizes can cause a lot of confusion to the novice buyer. Here are a few questions you can ask yourself before you buy anything:

- *I don't have a garden, but can I still feed birds?*
  The answer is yes! Feeders can be bought for all sorts of situations, including the

most urban of environments. If you live in a flat and don't have a garden, look for feeders that have suckers to attach to window glass. Always ensure that the feeder can be securely attached and will not be in danger of falling.

- *Will I regularly clean out my feeders?*
  We all have good intentions, but life sometimes gets in the way. If you think the answer is no, go for a low-maintenance, easy-to-clean option, like a steel mesh peanut feeder or fatballs.
- *Are there lots of squirrels about?*
  If the answer is yes, then you'll need a good squirrel-proof feeder. A metal cage around a feeder is one option, but this may stop larger birds from feeding, and Sparrowhawks have been known to attack birds inside the cage. Adding a baffle to the pole to stop the squirrels from running up will help. Also, some feeders have a protective sleeve which drops down when a squirrel lands on it, thus cutting off the food.
- *Are there cats in my garden?*
  If the answer is yes, try not to put too much food on the ground, and keep it away from cover where cats could be lurking.

The Best Bird-feeders

Nut feeders made of steel mesh are the best way to offer this food. The mesh size needs to be about 6 mm wide, as this is large enough not to harm beaks and small enough to stop whole nuts from being taken (whole nuts can choke young birds).

Peanuts in their shells; also called monkey nuts, these can be hung up on string, without the need for a feeder.

Seed feeders vary in size. The long plastic tubes are best, especially if they have a small tray at the base, but don't buy a huge one unless you have a very busy garden. Food that isn't eaten in time can get mouldy and will be left uneaten. Furthermore, it is important that the feeder can be taken apart for cleaning, as bad hygiene in feeders can be very dangerous to birds (see over) and, indeed, to humans.

Seed trays are an excellent way to get good views of birds feeding, but the wind can blow away the food. If you use mixed seed, messy eaters tend to tip out much of it in search of their favourite morsels. Rectangular wooden feeders with plastic sides can get messy quickly, and food tends to get stuck if you buy the cheaper mixes.

Fat feeders vary greatly, from the ready-made metal cages for pre-packed fat and seed blocks to the familiar fatball. It's really up to you how you want to offer this food, although making your own fat seed cake is often the cheaper option. As mentioned previously, if you are worried about birds trapping their feet or tongues in the surrounding mesh, remove it and use an alternative dispenser.

Hygiene is probably the single most important problem when feeding birds, and it is often overlooked. It is imperative that you regularly clean your bird-table and feeders with a mild disinfectant. Sick birds can leave behind bacteria, and mouldy food can contain toxins and so will be left uneaten. Droppings should never be allowed to accumulate on feeders. There is a very small risk of bird diseases being transferred to humans, so always make sure that you wash your hands after handling feeders. Furthermore, all feeders should be easy to take apart for cleaning, and should be done so regularly. Finally, remember that bird-tables don't last forever, and must be destroyed once they become too weathered to clean properly.

A GUIDE TO NESTBOXES

You may well ask why should we offer artificial accommodation for birds when they have been building their own homes for thousands of years. The answer to this question is that mature, broadleaf woodland has been largely destroyed over the centuries, and as a consequence, so have many of the natural nest-sites for hole-nesting species reliant on old trees. Creating an artificial woodland home in your garden not only encourages birds to breed, but also offers a great way to watch their secret lives unfold before your eyes.

Don't worry if you're not a natural at woodwork, as there are plenty of good nestboxes available from shops and on the Internet. If, however, you are tempted to make your own, and many people do, *The BTO Nestbox Guide* by Chris du Feu, (available from the BTO), offers great advice on the subject. See also the information available at http://www.bto.org/notices/nestbox_guide.htm.

There are some general rules to remember when installing nestboxes. These rules apply for all types of nestboxes, both large and small. With a little care and attention, it is possible to get up to six different species nesting within an average-sized garden. Finding the right home for the right bird needs a little knowledge, but once learned, you could have a buzzing nursery on your doorstep. There are various types of nestbox, and you will need to decide which of these are the most appropriate for the birds found in your garden..

- Ensure that the box is watertight from above, to keep the rain out. Just in case your box does leak, however, drilling some holes in the bottom for drainage is a good idea, and will help with ventilation generally.
- Make sure the box is well insulated. Wooden boxes should be made of wood that is at least 15 mm thick.
- Don't point the hole in the direction of the prevailing wind, as rain may be driven into the box.
- Don't place a box in direct sunlight, as birds can die if the box becomes an oven during the hotter part of the day.
- Security is vital. You must make sure the lid can't be lifted by cats or other predators. Putting a metal plate around the entrance hole will also deter woodpeckers and squirrels from attacking the hole to eat the nestlings (although woodpeckers will often make holes through the side of the box anyway).
- Location is very important. Don't put a box near to a feeding station, for example.
- Place the box at the relevant height for a particular species, remembering that some birds – such as Marsh and Coal Tits – like to nest near to the ground.
- Keeping the box clean helps prevent parasites, including fleas, from spreading.
- Towards the end of August (or autumn for multi-brooded species such as sparrows), empty out the box and clean it with boiling water (but never use bleach or detergent)

Enclosed Nestbox

This is very much the standard nestbox, and so in order to tailor-make it for different species, you need to look at the size of both the box itself and the entrance hole in particular. The measurements suggested below are minimum sizes; the first dimension refers to the height at the front, the second to the width, and the third to the depth of the box. The height of the hole above the base is the most important measurement, as it must prevent predators from reaching in to get at the young.

Small Enclosed Nestbox
(175 x 120 x 150mm)
- 25mm for Blue, Coal and Marsh Tits
- 28mm for Great Tits, Pied Flycatchers and Tree Sparrows
- 32mm for House Sparrows, Nuthatches and, occasionally, Lesser Spotted Woodpeckers

Larger Enclosed Nestbox
(250 x 150 x 180mm)
- 45 mm for Starlings
- 50 mm for Great Spotted Woodpeckers

Log Nestbox

This is basically a more natural-looking enclosed nestbox, so the same sizes for the entrance hole apply. These boxes can be either bought or self-made.

Open-fronted Nestbox

Similar to the enclosed type, but instead of a hole entrance, roughly half the frontage is left open. These boxes attract mainly Robins, Wrens and, occasionally, Pied Wagtails. Spotted Flycatchers also use them, but they prefer over half the frontage open. These boxes are used more rarely than the enclosed variety.

Bird-shelf
A simpler version of an open-fronted nestbox, this straightforward design is particularly attractive to Pied Wagtails, Spotted Flycatchers and Blackbirds.

Specialized Nestboxes
Some species of birds have such specific nesting requirements that they require specially adapted boxes which, generally-speaking, only they will use.

Bowl nestboxes are specially designed for *House Martins*, but *Swallows* will also use them. Martins usually nest in colonies, so putting up these boxes in pairs can help encourage multiple use. The boxes can have either side- or forward-facing entrance holes. If you are worried about the mess that can pile up from the birds' droppings, then fix a wooden tray underneath the nest. These nestboxes can be either hand-made or bought in shops or on the Internet.

Treecreeper: There is still some debate as to the effectiveness of this type of nestbox. Treecreepers normally nest in a natural nook or cranny behind bark, especially on soft-barked redwoods. However, the boxes are definitely worth a try, and fitting old bark to the outside of the box can increase the occupancy rate.

Kestrel: Generally speaking, Kestrels like to nest on cliff edges or ledges on buildings, always with an open aspect. To replicate this, the Kestrel box, a large open-fronted type, can be fixed to either trees, poles or buildings. The best sites are in quiet and undisturbed locations within reach of grassland for hunting. Tawny Owls have also been known to nest in these boxes.

Tawny Owl: As they like to nest in holes in trees, you can replicate this by buying or making long, thin boxes (ideally 795 x 230 x 230 mm). These should be fixed to a tree, either at an angle or

slung under a branch.
Conventional large-entrance-
holed boxes are also popular
with Tawnies. Whichever type
of box you use, it is worth
putting some wood chips in
the bottom to make the
birds feel at home.

Barn Owl: These birds adapt
readily to nestboxes and will even
use them throughout the year as roost-sites.
Boxes should be a minimum size of 450 x 450 x
750 mm and have a hole of at least 150 x 200 mm,
although bigger is fine. A square entrance of about 230 x 230
mm should be cut to the corner, and the front of the box should have a
lipped tray to allow the young owls to walk around or wait outside. The box should
be fixed securely on a pole, on a tree, or inside or outside a building, but never put
a box in a building where access could be cut off. You may find other species
occupying these larger boxes: Stock Doves, Little Owls and Jackdaws all favour
cavities and so will use these boxes, sometimes one after another in the same year.

WHAT TO DO WITH 'LOST' YOUNG BIRDS

Nestlings may be pink and naked, or covered in a fuzzy down.
Some may be just showing their development 'pin' feathers. The first
thing to do upon finding a nestling is to try to put it back in its nest. If
you can't find the nest, or it has been destroyed, then try making a
substitute nest (a small lined box or margarine tub with drainage holes will do) and put
it high up, close to where the nestling was found. There is a slim chance the parents will
return if they hear it begging for food. Nestling birds need constant parental care. If this
can't be delivered, their chances of survival are very slim.

Fledglings look like big-mouthed, scruffy versions of their parents. Their tails are
short and they often sit in a hunched-up pose. These birds have probably already
fledged, so putting them back in the nest won't help. Stay well back and watch to
see if the parents return with food. Parents can stay away for quite a while if they
are out hunting for food. Most of the time, the parents do return and manage to
coax the fledgling out of danger. This is by far the best scenario, as the majority of
birds who are hand-reared at this stage won't survive. But note: young Tawny Owls
sometimes sit on the ground; do not interfere with them, as they are perfectly
capable of climbing back up the tree to return to the nesting hole. If the adults don't
come back and you are absolutely sure the fledgling has been abandoned, and you
can't face letting nature take its course, then intervention is necessary.

If you decide to try hand-rearing, be prepared to offer round-the-clock care. You'll
need to identify the bird and work out the best food for it (the RSPCA should be able
to offer this advice). Try to
keep the bird outside, and
keep contact to the bare
minimum. The bird should be
released as soon as possible.
Finally, don't be too hard on
yourself if all your efforts fail:
it's rare for non-experienced
bird carers to succeed at
keeping a fledgling alive.

Here is a quick checklist of things to do:
- Place the bird in a cardboard box in a quiet place
- Try to identify the bird
- Seek expert advice from the RSPCA
- Keep contact to an absolute minimum
- Don't give it milk, as birds can't digest this
- Offer tinned cat or dog-food soaked in water

The Species

Mallard *Anas platyrhynchos*

Occurrence: All year round
Habitats: Anywhere near freshwater – ponds, ditches, streams etc
Garden ranking: RARE

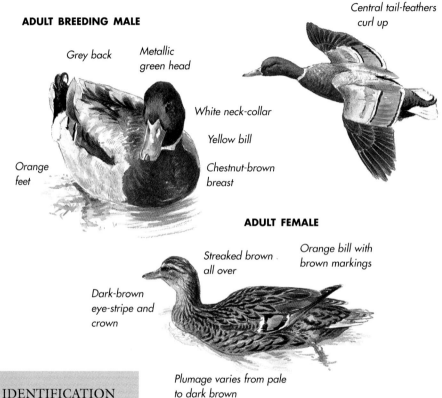

ADULT BREEDING MALE

Central tail-feathers curl up

Grey back

Metallic green head

White neck-collar

Yellow bill

Orange feet

Chestnut-brown breast

ADULT FEMALE

Streaked brown all over

Orange bill with brown markings

Dark-brown eye-stripe and crown

Plumage varies from pale to dark brown

IDENTIFICATION POINTS

- Male has metallic green head, white collar, brown breast
- Female streaked brown all over
- Dark blue speculum (panel in wing)
- Orange legs

CONFUSION SPECIES AND IDENTIFICATION NOTES

Mallards frequently interbreed with domestic ducks, and it is a common mistake to call every duck you see at the local pond or river a Mallard. In the wild there are a few female species that could be confusing: Gadwall, Shoveler (but not when you see their bill!) and the rare Black Duck from America.

CHARACTERISTICS
LENGTH: 50–65 cm
WINGSPAN: 81–98 cm
VOICE: Females: loud familiar 'quack, quack, quack'. Males offer a soft, nasal, whistling 'khraab' or 'raehb'.
NESTBOX: Yes.
NESTING: Wide range of nest-sites from trees to flowerbeds next to houses, but always in dense cover. Females take regular breaks while brooding, covering the eggs with their down. 8–12 grey-green eggs laid between February–October.
FOOD & FEEDING: A wide variety, ranging from acorns and berries while foraging on the ground, to water-snails, larvae, tadpoles and fish while in water. Ducklings zoom around on water and land snatching insects, which make up the bulk of their diet. Tame birds will take bread, cereal, grass pellets and grain.

Without doubt the Mallard is the most familiar and best-loved duck in Britain and probably Europe. Most domestic ducks are descended from the Mallard. The familiar 'quack-quack' call of the female and the ability to adapt to the urban environment means that many people come into contact with this bird. However, a wild Mallard is a completely different creature to the tame, semi-domesticated bird. They are incredibly shy and very wary of humans, so if you encounter one while out walking, you are unlikely to get very close.

Watching Mallard courtship can be a harrowing experience, especially where several males tirelessly harass a single female. Courtship can include bill dipping, tail shuffling and lots of intimate approaches. When she has had enough, the female will take off, usually with the males in hot pursuit.

Once the female is on the nest, the male begins to moult into what is known as eclipse plumage. During this moult, all of the flight-feathers are shed, making the bird look scruffy, unable to fly and more vulnerable to predators.

Red-legged Partridge *Alectoris rufa*

Occurrence: All year round
Habitats: Farmland, heaths and rural gardens
Garden ranking: RARE

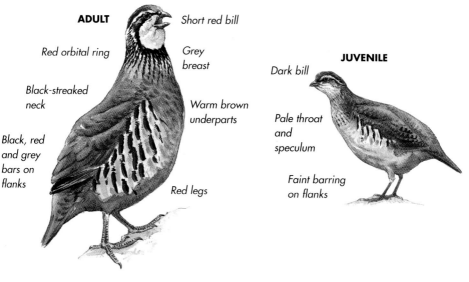

ADULT

Short red bill

Red orbital ring

Grey breast

JUVENILE

Dark bill

Black-streaked neck

Warm brown underparts

Pale throat and speculum

Black, red and grey bars on flanks

Faint barring on flanks

Red legs

Red-brown on corners of tail

Flies low to the ground with rapid wing-beats then stiff-winged glides

IDENTIFICATION POINTS
- Striking head pattern
- Barring on the flanks
- Very upright when running
- More likely to run than Grey Partridge

CONFUSION SPECIES AND IDENTIFICATION NOTES
The smaller Grey Partridge is the only other partridge in the UK. It lacks the strong contrasting head and flank patterns of the Red-legged. Instead, it has a brick-red head colour and males have an obvious dark-brown belly-patch.

CHARACTERISTICS
LENGTH: 32–34 cm
WINGSPAN: 47–50 cm
VOICE: Calls vary and include a hoarse series of chuffing 'kcho-kcho-kcho', followed by 'kochoko–koke kochoko-koke'.
NESTBOX: No.
NESTING: Grass-lined nest is well-hidden in dense foliage; male makes the initial scrape in the ground. Female sometimes lays two clutches of eggs in different places, one for herself and the other for the male to brood. If both broods succeed, parents will join forces, rearing all young together. 10–20 pale brown, red-spotted eggs laid between April–June.
FOOD & FEEDING: Spends much of the day scraping for seeds and roots. Eats the leaves of weeds, as well as slugs and insects – especially caterpillars.

Commonly referred to as the French Partridge, as this is where the British population originated. In the late 1700s thousands of chicks were imported to England and reared for their sporting value. It is now a common sight to see a family of Red-legged Partridges while walking in lowland farmland.

Although very good at hiding in long grass, if you get too close they are likely to run off at high speed.

A very beautiful bird; their fine markings and delicate demeanour make them welcome garden visitors. Although shy, they will come to the bottom of bird-tables in rural gardens to collect stray grain or seeds. They can adapt to a variety of habitats, ranging from heathland to rough wasteland, and will even venture into mountainous regions.

There are four similar-looking *Alectoris* partridges found in Europe, but their geographical range rarely overlaps.

25

Pheasant *Phasianus colchicus*

Occurrence: All year round
Habitats: Open countryside, farmland, hedgerows
Garden ranking: RARE

TORQUATUS has white neck collar

Head greenish-black with purple lustre

Grey rump and barred brown tail

COLCHICUS has no neck collar and warm brown rump

Rapid wing-beats during display

IDENTIFICATION POINTS
- Spectacular, iridescent plumage
- Long tail
- Males have bare red cheeks
- Some birds have white collars
- Most common game-bird in Europe

CONFUSION SPECIES AND IDENTIFICATION NOTES

Only another Pheasant could cause confusion. A lot of inter-breeding means birds vary. Lady Amherst's and Golden are two ornamental breeds that have escaped from estates and now roam freely and breed in some parts of the UK, although both are quite rare these days.

CHARACTERISTICS
LENGTH: 53–89 cm
WINGSPAN: 70–90 cm
VOICE: Alarm call (often when flushed) is a harsh rapid-fire 'kut-ork kut-ork-ok-ok'. During display male offers a short sharp 'koohrk-ut' followed by a drum of wing-beats then ruffled feathers. Females have a range of soft calls.
NESTBOX: No, but sometimes nests on straw bales.
NESTING: Female makes a shallow scrape, often well hidden in long grass or in the thick of bramble bushes. 8–15 olive-brown eggs are laid from March to July.
FOOD & FEEDING: A real variety of foods, from seeds, grain, buds, grasses and acorns to insects, snails and even lizards. They are keen and frequent garden guests and won't think twice about jumping up onto the bird-table.

This spectacular bird looks out of place in Britain or even in Europe. With its brilliant copper colours and iridescence, it looks like some sort of exotic escapee. In fact, Pheasants come originally from Asia, and were introduced to Britain as far back as the 11th or 12th century.

A very common sight in the countryside, they prefer forest edges, open cultivated farmland, thick hedges and copses. Gamekeepers across the UK rear and release millions of them to be shot for sport. Males are seen more often than females and if they are in an area where not shot, they can become surprisingly tame. You quite often see a male surrounded by several females; this is his harem, which he defends with passion.

Chicks stay with mum for up to ten weeks. Soft contact calls are often uttered to make sure they don't stray too far. They spend most of the day foraging for insects and plant food.

Grey Heron *Ardea cinerea*

Occurrence: All year round

Habitats: Anywhere near freshwater, ponds, ditches, streams and marshes

Garden ranking: RARE

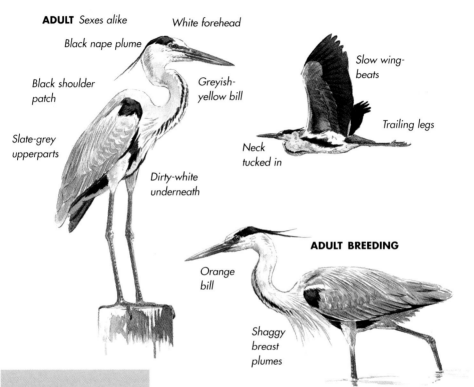

ADULT *Sexes alike*

White forehead

Black nape plume

Black shoulder patch

Greyish-yellow bill

Slate-grey upperparts

Dirty-white underneath

Slow wing-beats

Trailing legs

Neck tucked in

ADULT BREEDING

Orange bill

Shaggy breast plumes

IDENTIFICATION POINTS

- Tall grey, white and black bird
- Long, dagger-like bill
- In flight – arched, rounded wings,
- Slow wing-beat
- Flies with neck tucked in and legs trailing out past tail

CONFUSION SPECIES AND IDENTIFICATION NOTES

Not too many birds can be mistaken for a heron, although the following should be ruled out if you are unsure. A rare Purple Heron passing through on migration (if you are very lucky) and a Common Bittern in flight could also be confusing. Storks, Cormorants and cranes all fly with their necks out straight, unlike the Grey Heron.

28

CHARACTERISTICS
LENGTH: 90–98 cm
WINGSPAN: 175–195 cm
VOICE: Call is a loud, raucous 'kraank', often in flight. Various croaks at nest.
NESTBOX: No.
NESTING: Breeds colonially in 'heronries', usually in trees but sometimes reed-beds and cliffs. Female builds, male collects material for huge platform. Nests made of twigs. Can often see piles of white droppings stuck to the trees and ground below. The nest is used year after year, making it bigger each time. 3–5 pale blue eggs laid between February–July.
FOOD & FEEDING: Mostly fish and frogs, but will also take small mammals, insects, reptiles and even birds. Coastal birds will eat crabs.

If you have a garden pond with fish, then the chances are you will be all too familiar with this bird. They love to raid garden ponds, especially in spring when they have young to feed. For those of you that don't have a pond, the best place to watch herons is on wetland marshes, gravel pits, reservoirs, estuaries and rivers.

Herons can sit motionless for hours, but this patient hunter makes sudden, lightning-fast strikes with its dagger-like bill, pinpointing its powerless prey with great effect. A big winter freeze can be devastating for this handsome giant, as many die with no access to water and food; this is when your garden pond may just help them survive!

Juvenile herons are usually more compact than adults. They are grey-brown, with no marking on the head and no plumes.

Sparrowhawk *Accipiter nisus*

Occurrence: All year round
Habitats: Anywhere from small gardens to open countryside.
Garden ranking: UNCOMMON

MALE

Slate-grey upperparts

Rufous cheeks

Underparts rufous and barred

Piercing yellow eye

Grey tail with darker 4–5 darker bars

Thin, long yellow legs

25 per cent larger than male

Grey-brown upperparts

FEMALE

Underparts pale grey-brown with darker barring

JUVENILE Warm brown upperparts; coarse brown barring on pale underparts and bars on tail

IDENTIFICATION POINTS
- Male: grey back with rufous cheeks
- Female: much larger, usually lacking rufous colours
- In flight, blunt rounded wings are chunkier than kestrel
- Barring in flight on tail and belly

CONFUSION SPECIES AND IDENTIFICATION NOTES

If you're are a novice birdwatcher, it can be tricky to tell a Sparrowhawk from a Kestrel in flight. Remember that Kestrels have longer, thinner, more pointed wings, while Sparrowhawks have rounder, broader wings, look chunkier, and glide more. The obvious confusion species is the much larger (and rarer) Goshawk. However, Goshawks are unlikely to visit gardens, preferring large mature woodland. Merlins are similar but much smaller, and again, less likely to visit gardens.

CHARACTERISTICS

LENGTH: 28–38 cm

WINGSPAN: 55–70 cm

VOICE: Call is a harsh, rapid-fire 'kek-kek-kek'. Female's food-call a thin 'pii'.

NESTBOX: No.

NESTING: A new nest of twigs and sticks made every year. Broadleaf or conifer tree used. Nest built by female. Male brings food to brooding female. 3–6 bluish-white eggs between April–July.

FOOD & FEEDING: Small birds, including tits, finches and sparrows. Females can take larger birds up to size of Wood Pigeon. Bird-tables are a Sparrow-hawk's idea of fast food, so make sure your bird-table is near cover for a quick get-away.

Although Sparrowhawks are the masters of ambush, their short wings make them ideally suited to chase birds through dense woodland and hedges. Once caught, the prey is taken either to a plucking post or is eaten on the spot. They are commonly seen in early spring when performing their display flight, which includes soaring and slow-flapping. Broad rounded wings visible and obvious barring.

Like it or loathe it, the Sparrowhawk is now a common bird, with many visiting parks and gardens, especially feeders. During the 1950s and 60s, Sparrow-hawk numbers took a severe bashing, mainly due to agricultural poisoning. With strict controls now imposed, they have largely recovered, but remain vulnerable.

Sparrowhawks regularly hunt in gardens, and watching a Blue Tit being snatched from a bird-table can be upsetting. However, such incidents are all part of a natural eco-system in which Blue Tit and Sparrowhawk are integral components. Indeed, it is not thought that Sparrowhawks are responsible for the decline in recent decades of many of our common bird species. Cats, on the other hand, are an introduced predator and are known to kill many millions of garden birds, especially fledglings, every year.

Common Buzzard *Buteo buteo*

Occurrence: All year round
Habitats: Farmland, heaths, uplands and woodland edges
Garden ranking: RARE

ADULT MALE

Short neck

Medium to dark brown

Pale crescent on breast

Thickset body

Unfeathered yellow legs

Medium-length tail

Wings held in shallow 'V'

Fan-shaped tail when soaring

Fingered ends to wings

Broad, rounded wings

IDENTIFICATION POINTS
- Uniformly brown large bird of prey
- Holds wings in shallow 'V' when soaring
- Usually found over hilly, open farmland and woodland
- Often sits on telegraph poles
- Juveniles similar to adults but have streakier breast

CONFUSION SPECIES AND IDENTIFICATION NOTES

Many a tourist in Scotland has confused a distant Buzzard in flight with a Golden Eagle, even though the latter is twice the size and has more pronounced fingering on the ends of the wings. The tail and wing shape is also different. Put it this way, it's more likely that you're looking at a Buzzard than an eagle! Other buzzards, including Rough-legged and Honey, can be confusing, and Ospreys could be confused with pale-form Buzzards.

CHARACTERISTICS
LENGTH: 51–57 cm
WINGSPAN: 113–128 cm
VOICE: Call is a loud descending mewing whistle or 'piee-yay'.
NESTBOX: No
NESTING: Cliff ledges and trees are both used. A chunky nest is built or added to each year, made of sticks and lined with bracken or moss. The nest is returned to year after year. 2–4 bluish-white eggs with brown blotches, March–May. Both adults feed the young.
FOOD & FEEDING: A varied diet but mainly small mammals, including rabbits and voles. Carrion, birds, earthworms, insects and reptiles are also taken.

Once the Buzzard was a common sight throughout the whole of the Britain and Europe. Unlawful persecution, myxomatosis (which killed rabbits, the Buzzard's main prey) and agricultural poisoning seriously reduced their numbers, especially in eastern Britain. Thanks to the hard work of conservation organizations and some farmers, Buzzard numbers have risen again, making it currently the commonest bird of prey in the UK.

It is now a more familiar sight to see a Buzzard sitting on a post on the lookout for unsuspecting prey. Many rural gardens that back onto farmland will be familiar with this bird. They pose no threat to garden birds, and may even be a bonus – they help keep rabbits off vegetable patches.

Buzzards come in a variety of browns, and occasionally brown-grey, ranging from very dark (more common in Britain) to very pale, as shown above. The female is larger than the male.

Kestrel *Falco tinnunculus*

Occurrence: All year round.
Habitats: Anywhere from moorland, farmland and coastal areas to cities and
motorway verges
Garden ranking: RARE

FEMALE

Barred upper-
and underparts

Brown crown
and nape

6–7 dark bars
on tail

Slightly larger
than male

White tip to tail

MALE

Head bluish-
grey

Dark
moustachial
stripe

JUVENILE

Upper tail grey,
no bars

Dark band on
tip of tail

IDENTIFICATION
POINTS
• The only bird in UK to
  hover for long periods
• Often seen by roads
• Note long tail in flight
• Long, thin pointed
  wings

CONFUSION SPECIES AND IDENTIFICATION
NOTES
In flight, Sparrowhawk and Hobby. The similar-
looking Lesser Kestrel is found in southern Europe,
and is slightly smaller, more boldly marked on the
upperparts, and with a very different call.

CHARACTERISTICS

LENGTH: 32–35 cm

WINGSPAN: 71–80 cm

VOICE: Call is a rapid fire of short, sharp 'kee-kee-kee', especially at the nest. Also has a begging call – a high-pitched drawn-out 'kreee'.

NESTBOX: Yes. Open-fronted nestbox.

NESTING: A variety of nest-sites are used, ranging from holes in trees, rock ledges, buildings and old crow's nests. Nest consists of a scrape in the crown or loose collection of twigs or straw. 4–5 brown-blotched white eggs laid between April–June. Usually only one brood per year.

FOOD & FEEDING: Rodents (preferred food, especially voles), insects, beetles, earthworms, frogs and small birds. Will visit bird-tables, especially during winter months, where meat scraps and fat are taken. Garden birds occasionally taken.

In flight they look less bulky than Sparrowhawk, and the wings are thinner and more pointed. If you see a falcon hovering in the UK, it is most likely to be a Kestrel.

The Sparrowhawk has ousted the Kestrel as the most likely raptor to visit gardens. Most people see Kestrels as they hunt by the roadside using their characteristic hovering technique – it's not surprising that an old country name for the Kestrel is 'windhover'. Motorway and dual carriageway verges are kept cut short and can be full of wildlife, making them excellent places for Kestrels to hunt.

Following a decline, Kestrel populations seem to have stabilised recently, albeit at lower levels than in the 1970s. The fall in numbers may have been due to a lack of suitable habitat in the wider countryside for the small mammals on which they feed. More 'wildlife-friendly' farming may help the Kestrel, but meanwhile the Buzzard has overtaken it as the most common bird of prey in the UK.

Moorhen *Gallinula chloropus*

Occurrence: All year round
Habitats: Anywhere near freshwater – ponds, lakes, ditches etc
Garden ranking: RARE

ADULT

Upperparts tinged brown

Red bill and forehead

Black tail with central patch on white underside, held upright and flicked

Yellow tip to bill

Yellow-green legs

Underparts slate grey; white line on side

Flies low to ground

Legs trail behind body

JUVENILE

Pale face

White tail with dark centre

Underside pale brown

IDENTIFICATION POINTS
- Red forehead and bill with a yellow tip
- Jerky walk with flicking tail
- Longish yellow-green legs
- White line on sides
- White underside of tail

CONFUSION SPECIES AND IDENTIFICATION NOTES
Coots cause most confusion, but are black-grey all over with a large white forehead and bill. Juvenile Water Rails and Moorhens look similar, but Moorhen has a much shorter bill and a central black mark on underside of white tail.

CHARACTERISTICS
LENGTH: 32–35 cm
WINGSPAN: 50–55 cm
VOICE: Several different sounds from soft clucks to short, explosive 'kyorrl', or sharp 'ki-keck'.
NESTBOX: Will nest on artificial platforms put in large ponds.
NESTING: Both sexes build a platform nest of heaped vegetation on or near water, usually in good cover. 4–7 speckled brown eggs laid between March and September, but sometimes up to 20 as other females lay eggs in nest. Both adults rear young, and sometimes the young from earlier broods help feed the chicks.
FOOD & FEEDING: Wide variety, including plants and animals; seeds, grasses, berries, water plants, fish, snails, insects. Moorhens will readily steal food from other birds. Will feed from bottom of bird-table, delicately picking up any scraps it can find.

Moorhens are great birds to study. They may appear very nervous and unsure, but when you watch them for any length of time you realise how audacious they really are. If another Moorhen or unwelcome visitor intrudes on their territory, a fight will follow. These battles can be incredibly vicious yet stunningly acrobatic. Moorhens attack feet first, while repeatedly stabbing with their sharp bill.

Both parents tend their odd-looking offspring, which have a semi-bald red head with blue patches.

Very caring parents, Moorhens are highly devoted to their chicks. The young from a first brood will help their parents feed the next brood of chicks. Moorhens are not found on moors – their name comes from the Anglo-Saxon word 'mor', meaning bog or mere, hence their traditional country names of 'marsh hen' and 'bog bird'.

Black-headed Gull *Larus ridibundus*

Occurrence: All year round
Habitats: Everywhere, including coast, towns and farmland
Garden ranking: RARE

ADULT SUMMER
Dark chocolate hood
Dark red bill
Partial white eye-ring
Black tips on primaries
Dull red legs

ADULT WINTER
White head with two dark bars
Silver-grey upperparts
Orange bill with black tip
White underparts

FIRST WINTER Similar to adult winter but with more mottling on head and large amounts of brown on wings

FIRST SUMMER A mix of adult summer and first-winter plumage. Semi-formed hood flecked with white

IDENTIFICATION POINTS

- Small gull
- Chocolate-brown head when breeding
- White head with dark spot in winter
- Orange-red legs
- White leading edge to wings in flight
- Often seen inland, especially behind the plough in fields

CONFUSION SPECIES AND IDENTIFICATION NOTES

The chocolate hood in summer makes this species easier to identify, and this is the gull you are most likely to see inland. Similar – but rarer – gulls include the Little and the Mediterranean, both of which have black hoods during breeding season.

38

CHARACTERISTICS

LENGTH: 34–37 cm

WINGSPAN: 100–110 cm

VOICE: Calls include a harsh and repeated 'ky-eck', and a drawn-out 'kreeah'.

NESTBBOX: No.

NESTING: 3–6 brown-blotched eggs are laid between April–July. Breeds almost anywhere in large colonies, from inland sites to coastal edges. In UK they breed from south-east England northwards. Nests on the ground using loose vegetation.

FOOD & FEEDING: Almost anything from the bird-table. Eats a wide variety of food – insects, worms, carrion, fish and scraps from rubbish dumps.

This 'seagull' spends most of its time inland. The 'black-head' in its name is wrong as it's actually chocolate brown, and then only in summer. During the winter months it has a white head with nothing more than a dark spot behind the eye. Once you are able to identify them you can sit back and enjoy their intriguing social life.

They are highly gregarious; feeding, nesting and roosting all take place in groups that can be small or sometimes incredibly large. Inland breeding colonies range from less than 10 pairs to an amazing 20,000 pairs. They frequently visit gardens, most often in winter. If these gulls are in your neighbourhood, you'll have to get used to them swooping in and stealing food from other hungry birds.

In the cold winter months, noisy gangs of gulls will visit bird-tables more often. They're not fussy eaters and most things are taken. Their presence can deter smaller birds from feeding.

Common Gull *Larus canus*

Occurrence: All year round
Habitats: Anywhere, inland or coastal
Garden ranking: RARE

ADULT SUMMER

Bright white head and underparts

Dark, 'kind' eye

Black wing-tips with white spots

Yellow bill

Yellow-green legs

ADULT WINTER

Darker flecks on head and neck

Juveniles have mottled-brown backs and streaks on head and neck.

Dirty-yellow bill with dark mark

Dull yellow-green legs

IDENTIFICATION POINTS

- Medium-sized gull
- Looks 'kinder' than Herring Gull
- First-winter birds streaky brown
- Larger/stockier than Black-headed Gull
- Clearly smaller than Herring Gull

CONFUSION SPECIES AND IDENTIFICATION NOTES

The many plumages of younger gulls can make some novice bird-watchers nervous. The best thing is to remember that this bird is larger than a Black-headed and smaller than a Herring Gull. Also the dark, 'kind' eye makes this bird look friendly.

CHARACTERISTICS
LENGTH: 40–42 cm
WINGSPAN: 110–130 cm
VOICE: A mewing 'ke-ow', hence the name Mew Gull in North America. Alarm call a repeated 'gleeu-gleeu-gleeu'.
NESTBOX: No.
NESTING: Nests along freshwater coasts and sometimes miles inland on lakes, marshland or moors; even on roofs. 2–5 eggs laid between March–July, both parents rear young.
FOOD & FEEDING: Incredibly varied diet. It will kill and catch live prey. Insects, worms, carrion, berries, fish, crustaceans and anything from the kitchen bin!

If the Black-headed Gull should be called 'Chocolate-headed' then this bird should be the 'Not-so-common' Gull as both Herring and Black-headed are far more abundant! Common Gulls are most likely to be seen in the winter months when they stray away from their northern breeding sites and can sometimes be seen mingling with Black-headed Gulls inland, on farmland and playing fields.

Common Gulls breed in northern Europe, America, Russia and Asia. The best time to see them in any number in the UK is in March, when the wintering birds from Britain move up to their northern breeding sites. In the UK, they nest in Scotland, Western Ireland and northern England.

Lacks Black-headed Gull's leading white edge on wings

Black tips to primaries with large white 'mirror'

Feral Pigeon *Columba livia*

Occurrence: All year round
Habitats: An almost exclusively urban bird
Garden ranking: RARE

ADULT

Blue-grey

Red eye

Green patch

Pale grey back

Purple glossy neck

Two dark bars on wings

White rump

Feral pigeon same shape as Rock Dove, slightly fatter with varied plumages

IDENTIFICATION POINTS

- Most likely pigeon to be found in towns
- A cooing, moaning 'ooorr', 'ooorr'
- Vast plumage variation

CONFUSION SPECIES AND IDENTIFICATION NOTES

Feral Pigeons are domestic descendants of wild Rock Doves. Some look almost identical to their wild relatives, but the plumage varies greatly. Habitat is the best identification aid: Feral Pigeons live near humans, whereas Rock Doves prefer isolated cliffs and quarries in the north and west of Britain. However, feral birds are now returning to cliff-sites in increasing numbers, which is confusing the situation.

CHARACTERISTICS
LENGTH: 31–34 cm
WINGSPAN: 63–70 cm
VOICE: A cooing, moaning 'ooorr', 'ooorr'.
NESTBOX: Yes. Enclosed nestbox and dovecotes.
NESTING: Their ancestors nested on cliff edges; in towns, buildings with holes and ledges make ideal replacements.
FOOD & FEEDING: Spilt grain from horse nosebags have been replaced by fast-food waste in towns and cities. Mainly vegetarian, but also eats meat. Rock Doves feed on a variety of plants and crops.

Today's Feral Pigeons are a product of interbreeding between the many domestic varieties. The Ancient Egyptians were probably the first to domesticate them, and used pigeons to carry news of the coronation of Pharaoh Ramses III.

This successful bird's numbers have increased dramatically over the years, and for some city-dwellers they are nothing more than rats with wings. The link between the human and pigeon population may be an uncomfortable one, as the more waste we tip into the street, the more food pigeons have. Feral Pigeons breed whenever plenty of food is available, so the best way to control their numbers is to reduce urban waste. Courting males have no shame when it comes to seducing a mate, using pavements and gardens to perform their strutting courtship.

A courting male will relentlessly pursue his intended mate on the ground. He circles around her, with his neck feathers inflated and his tail spread, bowing and cooing with tenacious ardour.

Stock Dove *Columba oenas*

Occurrence: All year round
Habitats: Parks, wooded farmland, anywhere with mature trees
Garden ranking: RARE

ADULT

Blue-grey upperparts

Green patch on neck (not white, as in Wood Pigeon)

Two dark bars on wing

Rose-pink patch on chest

No white in wings

Grey rump

Broad tail band

Black tip to tail

JUVENILE

Dark bill

No white in wings

IDENTIFICATION POINTS
- No white patch on neck
- Smaller than Wood Pigeon
- No white on wings in flight
- Dark edge to wings in flight
- Pale grey underwings in flight

CONFUSION SPECIES AND IDENTIFICATION NOTES
Wood Pigeons and Rock Doves/Feral Pigeons can be confusing. Stock Doves are smaller than Wood Pigeons and have a shorter tail (roughly the size of the Feral Pigeon's). Unlike the Wood Pigeon, they have no white on the neck or in the wings. Juveniles of both species look similar, but the Stock Dove is more delicate and lacks the white in wing.

CHARACTERISTICS
LENGTH: 32–34 cm
WINGSPAN: 63–69 cm
VOICE: Repetitive moaning 'ooo-woo', getting faster as it goes.
NESTBOX: Yes.
NESTING: Holes are favoured sites, whether in trees, boxes, cliffs or buildings. Has been known to nest in old rabbit holes. Not much material used. 2 eggs laid between February–November, both parents brood and rear young.
FOOD & FEEDING: Vegetarian, with seeds being mainstay of diet. Also plant material like buds, dock and buttercup. Harvest-time sees many Stock Doves feeding on grain spillage. Unlikely to visit bird-tables, but will feed on garden plants and spilt seeds. Will occasionally eat insects.

This shy, elusive bird is probably one of our most over-looked, and is commonly written off as 'just another Wood Pigeon'. However, on closer inspection you can see the beauty and elegance of this unassuming bird. Its blue-grey plumage with soft, rose-pink coloured breast looks so smooth it could have been air-brushed.

Stock Doves have an impressive display flight. Males and females glide around each other while holding their wings in a shallow 'V' shape. Occasionally they clap their wings while in mid-flight, and the distinctive sound this makes means that love is in the air!

They are widespread over Europe but absent from the far north of Scotland and Scandinavia. Although they tend to be more solitary than Wood Pigeons, they do join forces and feed together in the winter. When seen side-by-side, the size and plumage differences are obvious. The best viewing-time is early spring, when they perform their distinctive display flight.

Wood Pigeon *Columba palumbus*

Occurrence: All year round
Habitats: Everywhere. Woods, parks, gardens, cities etc
Garden ranking: COMMON

ADULT

White and green
neck patch

Ash-grey
upperparts

Lilac-coloured
breast

Dark
primaries

Dark tail
band

Long
tail

Dark eye

Dark bill

Warm grey
upperparts

JUVENILE

White edge
to wing

Orange-
brown chest

IDENTIFICATION
POINTS
• Fat, grey bird with
pinkish breast
• White mark on neck
and wings
• Europe's largest
pigeon
• Most common pigeon
in countryside

CONFUSION SPECIES AND IDENTIFICATION
NOTES
Stock Dove, Feral Pigeon, Rock Dove. However, the
Wood Pigeon is bigger than all these birds. The white
markings on the wings and neck are distinctive.

CHARACTERISTICS

LENGTH: 40–42 cm

WINGSPAN: 75–80 cm

VOICE: A throaty, cooing 'wha-hoo, hoo', repeated quickly 3 to 7 times. Also a soft 'blowing' 'doo-doooh, doo doo-du'.

NESTBOX: No.

NESTING: Normally in trees, but will use buildings. Scrappy platform twig-nest made by both parents. 2 white eggs are laid between February–November.

FOOD & FEEDING: Mainly vegetarian, but will eat insects. Cultivated crops: cereals, peas, beans, cabbages, turnips, swedes. Also beechmast, acorns, haws, flower-buds etc. Parents feed squabs a protein-rich milk made in their crop. This means pigeons are not so insect-dependent as other birds. A clumsy visitor to the bird-table; prefers to eat on the ground. Very nervous.

This bulky giant of a pigeon doesn't walk or hop – it waddles; its legs and feet seem far too small for its body, making it look ungainly on the ground. Amazingly, its feathers weigh more than its bones. It is a huge pest to  arable farmers and even gardeners are wary of large numbers; they can form huge flocks which plunder food from fields or allotments. In the UK, the Wood Pigeon is non-migratory, so can cause crop damage throughout the year; worse still, numbers increase when others arrive from northern Europe in autumn. They are incredibly successful birds, with the UK population doubling over the past 25 years, and they are now a common garden bird.

During breeding time Wood Pigeons have an impressive display flight. They make a steep climb, clap their wings, then glide down with their tail spread. This is seen early on in the year, usually in February or March.

Collared Dove *Streptopelia decaocto*

Occurrence: All year round
Habitats: Everywhere from cities to farmland, but absent from uplands
Garden ranking: VERY COMMON

ADULT *Sexes alike*

Dark, 'kind' eye

Black half-ring
on neck

Pink wash on
breast

Pale grey-brown
upperparts

Dark primaries

Broad white mark
end of tail

Dark
primaries

Uniform grey
underside of wings

IDENTIFICATION
POINTS
- Black partial neck-collar
- Pale buff-grey colour
- Dainty, elegant bird
- Often seen in pairs

CONFUSION SPECIES AND IDENTIFICATION
NOTES
The summer-visiting Turtle Dove is similar in shape but has a completely different plumage – orange-brown back with dark centres to feathers, grey head and a dark tail. It also has thinner, more pointed wings in flight.

CHARACTERISTICS
LENGTH: 31–33 cm
WINGSPAN: 47–55 cm
VOICE: A soft, throaty cooing 'doo-dooo-do'. Also a call that sounds like a genteel Victorian lady saying 'ooooh'!
NESTBOX: No.
NESTING: A precarious-looking flimsy nest made by female in trees and sometimes buildings. Males collect nesting material. 2 white eggs brooded by both parents. Nesting between February–November. Up to 6 broods known per year.
FOOD & FEEDING: Mainly vegetarian, but will eat insects such as caterpillars and aphids. Main food is seeds, grain and fruit. Squabs are fed pigeon milk by parents. Will visit bird-tables to eat seeds and grain, but very nervous.

The Collared Dove's ancestral home is hot, dry, dusty Central Asia. It has spread with unbelievable speed through Europe, reaching the UK in the 1950s. They favour warmer human environments, like villages, towns, cities and farmyards, and have found an ideal ecological niche to exploit. Unlike many other birds, the Collared Dove doesn't rely on insects to feed to its young – this could be one reason for its impressive success story.

Their elegance and gentle nature make them very endearing birds; they pair for life and are commonly seen in couples. During winter they form large flocks. Garden birdwatchers can build up a close relationship with their resident Collared Doves; with patience, they will feed readily from the hand and even fly down to your feet to ask for food.

JUVENILE

No neck mark

Pale, washed-out plumage

Turtle Dove *Streptopelia turtur*

Occurrence: Summer visitor to England and Wales, May–September.
Habitats: Cultivated countryside, deciduous woods, mature hedgerows
Garden ranking: RARE

ADULT

Grey forehead,
crown, nape

Buffy-pink face

Black bars
white behind

Pink-grey breast

JUVENILE

No neck markings,
generally duller

No pink breast

IDENTIFICATION
POINTS
- Small, slim dove
- Eye surrounded by
  bare red skin
- Long, pointed wings
  in flight
- White edge to
  darker tail
- Warm chestnut back

Flight is very different
from Collared Dove,
faster and more fitful

Diamond-
shaped tail

White edge
to darker tail

CONFUSION SPECIES AND IDENTIFICATION
NOTES
Collared Dove has similar shape and Kestrel has
similar colouring but is larger.

50

CHARACTERISTICS
LENGTH: 26–28 cm
WINGSPAN: 47–53 cm
VOICE: Deep and quiet purring 'turrrrr-turrrrr-turrr', repeated several times.
NESTBOX: No.
NESTING: 2 pinkish-white eggs are laid in a well-hidden but frail-looking nest. Tends to nest lower in trees than other doves/pigeons. Both parents brood and rear young, feeding them pigeon's milk, which the young take from their parents' throat.
FOOD & FEEDING: Mainly seeds from plants, especially weeds. Joins poultry to eat grain on farms. As they are so shy, they are unlikely to visit the bird-table. However, big gardens with mature trees and unkempt shrubs may attract them.

These beautiful and elegant birds have declined in numbers alarmingly in recent years, due to a range of factors. During our winter they live in sub-Saharan Africa, returning to breed in Europe every summer. On their way to and fro they risk being shot by hunters in France and the Mediterranean, and when they get back here there are too few mature hedgerows or weed-rich fields to support them. Even in their African winter homes, drought and deforestation puts them at risk. It can be frustratingly difficult to get a good long view of these shy birds, as they tend to fly off as soon as they are spotted.

The 'turtur' in the Turtle Dove's scientific name refers to the 'turrr-turrr' call and has nothing to do with turtles or tortoises.

51

Cuckoo *Cuculus canorus*

Occurrence: Summer visitor, April–September
Habitats: A huge range, from moorland to woodland edge and farmland.
Garden ranking: RARE

Yellow orbital ring

Long, thin
grey bill

Grey
upperparts

Grey chest

Wings drooped
at rest

MALE

Barred
underparts

Flies low and enters
cover at speed

FEMALE

Two colour phases
are known for
females : rufous
and grey

Holds body
horizontally

Faint barring
on breast and
throat

Wings not
raised above
body

Pointed
wings

JUVENILE

White marks
in wings

Grey-brown

Heavily barred with
white nape patch

IDENTIFICATION POINTS

- Overall grey with pale underparts
- Long, pointed wings
- Looks like small raptor in flight
- Droops wings when perched

CONFUSION SPECIES AND IDENTIFICATION NOTES

In flight they can look like falcons such as Kestrel, Hobby or Merlin.

52

CHARACTERISTICS
LENGTH: 32–34 cm
WINGSPAN: 55–60 cm
VOICE: Male: familiar sounding 'cuc-ooo'; female: explosive, bubbling chuckle.
NESTBOX: No.
NESTING: No nest made, as it uses other birds' nests. Favourite nests are Reed Warbler, Dunnock and Meadow Pipit, but has been known to use the nests of nearly 100 other species. Lays one egg in each hijacked nest, up to as many as 25 per season. Cuckoos tend to use nests of the species that brought them up.
FOOD & FEEDING: Insects, especially poisonous, hairy caterpillars that other birds don't take. Butterflies (Large White seem to be a favourite), beetles, flies etc. They may eat the egg removed from host's nest and have also been known to eat chicks from nests.

Whatever you feel about the Cuckoo, you have to admire the way it reproduces without any hassle or responsibility. Its parental duties involve finding a suitable nest, removing an egg and laying its own. That's it! After they've finished, they are free to prepare for the long flight back to Africa, assured that their chick is being cared for. As soon as the young Cuckoo has hatched, it pushes out all other eggs or chicks, to ensure it gets its foster-parents' undivided attention.

However, it's not all plain sailing for the Cuckoo. Their numbers have been steadily declining since the 1940s, and this highly insectivorous bird may be suffering from habitat loss, insecticide use and recent climate change, which has led to wetter, colder springs and summers.

Rufous-phase female at nest

53

Barn Owl *Tyto alba*

Occurrence: All year round
Habitats: Open country, farmland, forest edges, coastal marshes
Garden ranking: RARE

ADULT *Sexes similar*

Black eye

Heart-shaped face

Dark line around heart-shaped mask

GUTTATA race

Grey-brown upperparts

Upperparts rich yellow-brown with grey flecks

Long feathered legs

Underparts warm brown

Short tail

Powerful toes with large talons

Ghostly, buoyant flight

Appears very pale

The pounce: head and feet first with wings held straight up

IDENTIFICATION POINTS
- Appears white in flight
- Frequently seen at dawn and dusk
- Long wings, short tail in flight
- Sits on fence posts

CONFUSION SPECIES AND IDENTIFICATION NOTES

As it's the only white owl you're likely to see, it can't be confused with others. In twilight, at first glance you might think it's a seagull. However, the flat face, wedge-shaped body and rounder wings soon become obvious.

54

CHARACTERISTICS
LENGTH: 33–35 cm
WINGSPAN: 85–93 cm
VOICE: Alarm call, often given in flight, is a shrill squeal. 'Song' is a drawn-out, eerie shriek, 'shreeee'. Begging call of young is a wheezy snoring, plus hissing and bill snapping if disturbed.
NESTBOX: Yes. Open-fronted ledge nestbox.
NESTING: Will nest throughout the year, usually 2 broods. No nest made but lays up to 6 almost spherical bright white eggs on old pellets. Nests in enclosed spaces, hollow trees, ledges in buildings and special Barn Owl nestboxes.
FOOD & FEEDING: Small mammals such as mice, voles and shrews. And sometimes rats. Will also take roosting birds and has been known to catch bats.

Despite the use of its blood-curdling screech on TV horror shows, the Barn Owl is still a popular bird – seeing one is always an exciting and uplifting experience. These cosmopolitan, ghost-like owls are the most widespread of all land birds: they are found on every continent apart from Antarctica.

Young Barn Owls are small noisy bundles of white fluff.

The *alba* in their scientific name means 'white', but the *guttata* race, from continental Europe and sometimes seen in the UK, is browner with a darker back. Their diurnal hunting makes them easy to see, with dusk and dawn the best times to look. Although they're not common, and have suffered from habitat loss, barn conversions and rodenticides, numbers are gradually increasing in many parts of Britain.

Little Owl *Athene noctua*

Occurrence: All year round
Habitats: Open country, farmland, forest edges in England and Wales,
but absent from Scotland and Ireland
Garden ranking: RARE

ADULT *Sexes alike*

White line
around face

Flat-looking head
with yellow eyes
and broad white
'eyebrows'

Pale flesh-
coloured bill

White
spots on
crown and
upper-parts

White
feathered
legs

JUVENILE

No spots on crown

Plain
underparts

Fast, undulating flight

Rounded wings

IDENTIFICATION
POINTS
• UK's smallest owl
• Active during the day
• Yellow eyes
• Brown with white
  spots

CONFUSION SPECIES AND IDENTIFICATION
NOTES
There are no other similar species in the UK. When
seen during the day it may look like a Mistle Thrush
in flight. Tends to sit low in shrubs and bushes, or sits
up proud on fence posts. General appearance is
small and squat, with a flat-looking head.

CHARACTERISTICS
LENGTH: 21–23 cm
WINGSPAN: 54–58 cm
VOICE: A sharp 'kee-ew'. Alarm call, a high-pitched 'chi-chi-chi'. Song is a soft low-pitched 'cooo-ek'.
NESTBOX: Yes.
NESTING: No nest is made; 3–5 white eggs laid April–July on the floor of enclosed space, e.g. hollow tree, old building or rabbit hole. Nest-sites are used repeatedly. Both parents feed young.
FOOD & FEEDING: Worms, insects (especially beetles), small mammals and birds. Will run after prey.

Athene, the Greek goddess of wisdom, adopted this bird as her emblem, recognizing its intelligence and quiet ferocity. Although mainly feeding on insects and worms, it will also tackle prey its own size, using its strong and powerful talons.

British Little Owls were introduced from Holland in the late nineteenth century. Apart from a dip in the 1960s, due to the impact of agro-chemicals, their numbers are now stable across Europe.

When disturbed, Little Owls normally fly only a short distance, with a characteristic bounding flight. If alarmed or curious, they stretch their neck, swing their body from side-to-side, then bob their head, even turning it upside down if especially agitated.

Hunting takes place at night, twilight and even during the day if feeding young. Food is taken mainly from the ground, and if necessary Little Owls can run down their prey.

57

Tawny Owl *Strix aluco*

Occurrence: All year round
Habitats: Mainly mixed or deciduous woodland, but also in large trees in towns,
parks and wooded gardens
Garden ranking: RARE

Sexes alike

Large, rounded
head

**ADULT RUFOUS
FORM**

Pale crown
stripes

White lines
on scapulars

Buff-
coloured
face

**ADULT
GREY
FORM**

Black eye

Barred tail

Grey-brown all over
paler breast with
grey flecks

Rounded wings

Square tail wings held
slightly downward

IDENTIFICATION POINTS

- Wood Pigeon-sized
- Predominantly brown
- Familiar 'to-wit-to-woo' and 'kew-vit' calls

CONFUSION SPECIES AND IDENTIFICATION NOTES

Long- and Short-eared Owls look similar in flight, but the former is scarce and the latter unlikely in gardens. Tawny is the commonest garden owl, and there are two colour forms, rufous and grey; the rufous is the more frequent.

CHARACTERISTICS

LENGTH: 37–39 cm

WINGSPAN: 94–104 cm

VOICE: Call of male is a familiar 'hooo-hoo-hooo', used for courtship and territory; female version softer and more hoarse. A sharp 'kew-vit' call is also used in alarm and can be quickly repeated. Young beg with a hissing 'ke-sip'.

NESTBOX: Yes, uses specially designed nestbox.

NESTING: Enclosed spaces, either man-made or natural, sometimes old magpie nests. 3–4 white eggs laid between late February–June. Female broods young for first fortnight, while male brings food to nest. Then both parents feed young.

FOOD & FEEDING: Small mammals, especially voles, mice and shrews. Town owls take more birds, usually at dusk. They will snatch brooding birds from nests and while at roost. May grab feeding birds at bird-tables, and severe weather can also force them to feed from the table. Also eats frogs and, more rarely, fish, snatched from the water's surface.

Britain's commonest owl, it is widespread throughout Europe but absent from Ireland. Spotting these birds is not so easy, however. Look out for a noisy group of angry birds, usually tits and finches, mobbing a silhouette in a tree. If an owl's daytime roost is discovered, small birds will noisily annoy it until it moves on.

If disturbed, Tawny Owls will stretch themselves as thin as possible, becoming almost invisible. They can also puff out their feathers in an impressive threat display to ward off intruders to the nest. During the start of their breeding season they can be very vocal during the day. Hoots and 'kew-vit' contact calls are common, but even when standing right next to the tree, they are still incredibly difficult to see.

The babies become fledglings in 28 to 37 days and depend on their parents for food for up to three months after leaving the nest.

Swift *Apus apus*

Occurrence: April–August
Habitats: Almost anywhere from rural to urban
Garden ranking: LESS COMMON

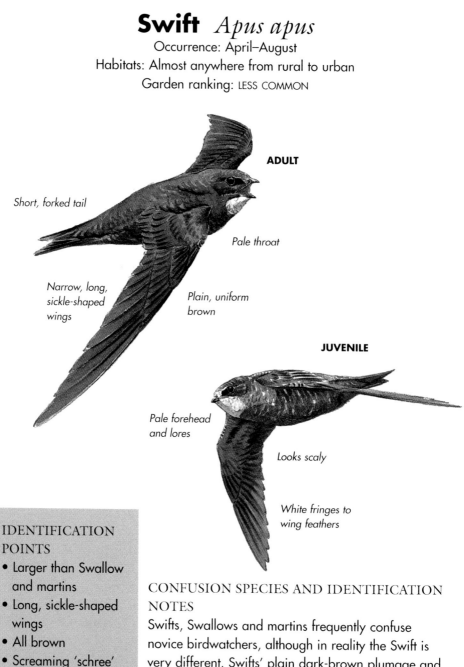

ADULT

Short, forked tail

Pale throat

Narrow, long, sickle-shaped wings

Plain, uniform brown

JUVENILE

Pale forehead and lores

Looks scaly

White fringes to wing feathers

IDENTIFICATION POINTS

- Larger than Swallow and martins
- Long, sickle-shaped wings
- All brown
- Screaming 'schree' calls

CONFUSION SPECIES AND IDENTIFICATION NOTES

Swifts, Swallows and martins frequently confuse novice birdwatchers, although in reality the Swift is very different. Swifts' plain dark-brown plumage and long sickle-shaped wings are obvious. The larger Hobby resembles the shape of the Swift in flight.

CHARACTERISTICS

LENGTH: 16–17 cm

WINGSPAN: 42–48 cm

VOICE: Shrill screaming 'schreee'. Excitable flocks fly in tight formation, screaming over the rooftops.

NESTBOX: Yes. An oblong box with a hole underneath will encourage nesting, and special brick boxes can be purchased.

NESTING: Nesting materials – grasses, feathers, leaves – are collected in the air then cemented together with saliva. Rock-faces are traditional nest-sites, although buildings are now mainly used. 2 or 3 white eggs are laid between May–August. Eggs hatch at staggered intervals to aid survival; chicks can survive over a week without food.

FOOD & FEEDING: Insects and airborne spiders, with all food caught on the wing. A staggering 10,000 insects can be taken in one day.

With a life on the wing – eating, hunting, sleeping and mating – these birds have become aerial geniuses. Unable to perch, they can only cling with their four strong claws to vertical eaves or rock ledges. If they land on the ground their wings are too long and too close to the ground for them to be able to take off again. If you find one stranded, you can help by throwing it up into the air.

With the possible exception of the albatrosses, no bird family spends more time on the wing than the swifts. Tremendous acrobats, their aerial exploits never cease to amaze – they even mate on the wing.

Their tiny beaks have a very wide gape, enabling them to scoop up large mouthfuls of insects, like an aerial trawler. Their amazing wings allow them to glide for long periods, saving energy. As soon as the young fledge they become independent and begin their long journey to their African winter quarters.

Kingfisher *Alcedo atthis*

Occurrence: All year round
Habitats: Near slow-moving freshwater, normally in lowland areas.
Absent from Northern Scotland
Garden ranking: RARE

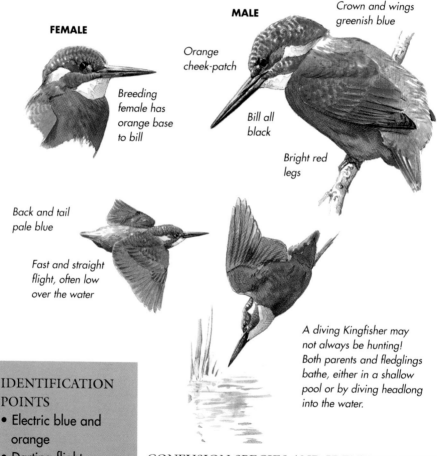

FEMALE

MALE

Crown and wings greenish blue

Orange cheek-patch

Breeding female has orange base to bill

Bill all black

Bright red legs

Back and tail pale blue

Fast and straight flight, often low over the water

A diving Kingfisher may not always be hunting! Both parents and fledglings bathe, either in a shallow pool or by diving headlong into the water.

IDENTIFICATION POINTS

- Electric blue and orange
- Darting flight
- Loud, shrill call in flight
- Large head
- Dagger-like bill

CONFUSION SPECIES AND IDENTIFICATION NOTES

Virtually unmistakable; there are no other birds similar to the Kingfisher in Britain, but beware if you see it head-on and facing you: its chest can appear dark chestnut in bad light.

CHARACTERISTICS
LENGTH: 16–17 cm (including 4 cm bill length)
WINGSPAN: 24–26 cm
VOICE: A loud, shrill piping 'chreee' or 'chee-kee'.
NESTBOX: No, but will nest in artificial earth banks.
NESTING: Usually in soft banks close to slow moving water. Both parents dig a one-metre-long, downward-sloping tunnel. 5–7 glossy white eggs are laid between April–August in nest chamber at end.
FOOD & FEEDING: Fish, aquatic insects, tadpoles and molluscs. Adults need to eat up to 12 small fish a day. Perches motionless in vegetation, then drops down with speed into water to grab prey.

Unfortunately, its shy nature and secretive behaviour mean that this stunningly attractive and exotic-looking bird is rarely seen, and even then only as a dazzling dart of electric blue dashing down a river, giving its shrill piping cry as it flies. But find its regular fishing posts, and good views become possible.

Prolonged freezes and water pollution are the two major dangers Kingfishers face. Ice means they simply can't feed, and their water needs to be clean to support a healthy population of fish. In the UK recent work to clean up rivers has helped the Kingfisher, but elsewhere in Europe the picture is not so good.

Both parents feed their young for the first few days after leaving the nest.

Green Woodpecker *Picus viridis*

Occurrence: All year round
Habitats: Lowland deciduous and mixed woodland, pastures, parklands and gardens with large lawns. Absent from Ireland
Garden ranking: RARE

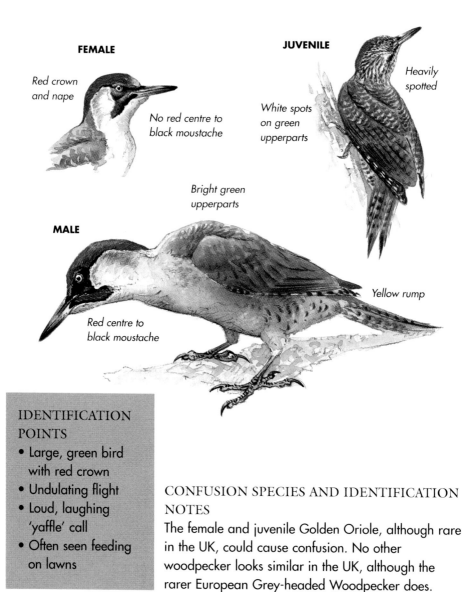

FEMALE

Red crown and nape

No red centre to black moustache

JUVENILE

Heavily spotted

White spots on green upperparts

Bright green upperparts

MALE

Yellow rump

Red centre to black moustache

IDENTIFICATION POINTS
- Large, green bird with red crown
- Undulating flight
- Loud, laughing 'yaffle' call
- Often seen feeding on lawns

CONFUSION SPECIES AND IDENTIFICATION NOTES
The female and juvenile Golden Oriole, although rare in the UK, could cause confusion. No other woodpecker looks similar in the UK, although the rarer European Grey-headed Woodpecker does.

64

CHARACTERISTICS
LENGTH: 31–33 cm
WINGSPAN: 40–42 cm
VOICE: Laughing, loud almost hysterical call 'yaah-yaah-yaah', known as 'yaffling'.
NESTBOX: Yes. Will use large enclosed boxes.
NESTING: 2–3 weeks taken to excavate nest in suitable tree between April–July. 5–7 white eggs laid and incubated by both parents. One brood only.
FOOD & FEEDING: Ants (eggs, pupae, adults) are favourite food and are extracted from cavities by the long, sticky tongue. Can eat up to 2000 ants a day, and often hunts for them on lawns. Beetles, grubs, caterpillars and bees are also eaten. Fatty scraps can tempt them to the bird-table, but rarely.

The UK's largest, most colourful woodpecker is about the size of a Jackdaw, and painfully shy. There are around 15,000 pairs breeding in Britain but finding them can be tricky, although their far-carrying laughing call often gives them away. Unlike the Great and Lesser Spotted Woodpeckers, they don't display by drumming on trees and will only hammer to excavate a nest-hole.

Green Woodpecker survival is linked to the availability of ants and much of each day is taken up looking for ant nests. When pastures were left unploughed and untouched by fertilizers, ants were prolific, but nowadays there is less suitable habitat. Despite this, numbers of Green Woodpeckers have generally increased across most of its range. Ants are not just a chief food source – to help clean its feathers, a Green Woodpecker will spread its wings over an ant's nest and wait for them to attack and angrily squirt formic acid. This acts as an insecticide, and once suitably cleansed, the woodpecker will preen itself clean of the ants.

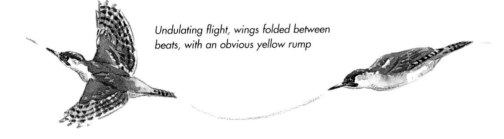

Undulating flight, wings folded between beats, with an obvious yellow rump

65

Great Spotted Woodpecker
Dendrocopos major

Occurrence: All year round
Habitats: Almost anywhere with trees: parks, gardens, woods. Absent from Ireland.
Garden ranking: UNCOMMON

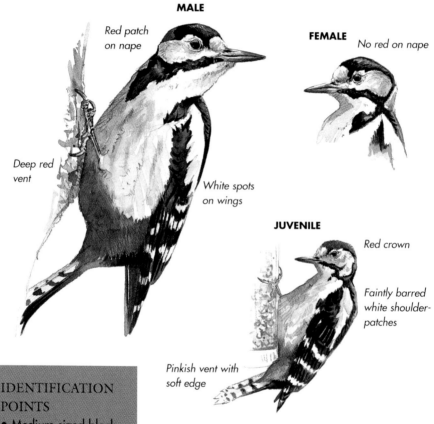

MALE

Red patch on nape

FEMALE
No red on nape

Deep red vent

White spots on wings

JUVENILE

Red crown

Faintly barred white shoulder-patches

Pinkish vent with soft edge

IDENTIFICATION POINTS
• Medium-sized black and white woodpecker
• White wing patches on back
• Red nape (males)
• Loud, sharp 'kick kick' call, often in flight

CONFUSION SPECIES AND IDENTIFICATION NOTES
The Lesser Spotted Woodpecker looks similar but is much smaller (roughly the size of a sparrow), while the Great Spotted is the size of a Song Thrush.

66

CHARACTERISTICS
LENGTH: 22–23 cm
WINGSPAN: 34–39 cm
VOICE: Short, sharp 'kick kick' call, whereas the song is made by drumming on bark. Each burst has around 10 taps delivered per second.
NESTBOX: Yes, large enclosed nestboxes.
NESTING: Both parents excavate nest, usually up to around five metres above ground level. 4–7 white eggs laid between April–July. One brood only.
FOOD & FEEDING: Insects are main food in the summer, including wood-boring beetles, which it excavates with its strong bill, then retrieves with its sticky tongue. In winter, nuts and seeds are the main food; especially likes peanut feeders.

Starlings are quick to capitalise on the woodpeckers' hard work. If they can, they will evict the builders and take over the nest-site.

These are exciting birds to watch in the breeding season, chasing around noisily at high speed through the trees. The male will spiral around a tree trunk in rapid pursuit of the female, followed by a mutual display flight, fluttering from tree to tree. In late winter or early spring both sexes will use resonant branches to drum on, marking territory and hoping to attract a mate.

In winter they will crash onto a peanut feeder, flushing off other birds, although a Blue Tit may stay put and open its beak in defiance. They like both coniferous and deciduous trees, eating the wood-boring insects that live behind the bark, smashing through or prising it away with their strong beaks. These colourful garden birds will even sometimes attack nestboxes and eat young tit fledglings.

Lesser Spotted Woodpecker
Dendrocopos minor

Occurrence: All year round
Habitats: Deciduous woodland, parklands, orchards and established hedgerows across Europe. Absent from Ireland and Scotland.
Garden ranking: RARE

MALE

Red crown

Barred back

Fawn cheek

Similar size to sparrow

FEMALE

Juveniles resemble adults but have a buff wash to the face, with a white forehead with black flecks; also spotty flanks.

Sharp bill

No red on crown

IDENTIFICATION POINTS
- Small; just bigger than sparrow
- Black and white all over
- Undulating flight

CONFUSION SPECIES AND IDENTIFICATION NOTES
Great Spotted Woodpecker looks similar but is much bigger (size of a Song Thrush), with a much longer, stronger bill.

CHARACTERISTICS
LENGTH: 14–15 cm
WINGSPAN: 25–27 cm
VOICE: Call is a shrill series of 'kee-kee-kee', similar to Kestrel. Alarm call is a soft 'chick', quieter than a Great Spotted. Drumming also softer and quieter.
NESTBOX: Yes. 32-mm-hole.
NESTING: The nest is excavated by both parents in almost any deciduous tree (birch and alder are favourites), sometimes even a fence post. 3–8 white eggs laid between April–July. Both parents incubate eggs.
FOOD & FEEDING: Insects are the main food, especially beetles and grubs that live in wood. Also aphids, moths, ants and flies. They will also eat fruit in winter. Very rare visitors to the bird-table, but will take seeds.

This tiny woodpecker doesn't always behave like other woodpeckers. It will join tit flocks in winter, fluttering around high in the tops of trees and along very thin branches. It will even forage along hedgerows and scrub quite close to the ground.

There are only between 3–6000 pairs in Britain and the numbers are dropping – Dutch Elm Disease and the loss of broadleaf woodland are two reasons for this. Their interesting courtship involves the male drumming to attract a female, who flies over, spreading her wings and tail, while the male quivers his wings and ruffles his crown. He then gives chase, high in the trees and with a moth-like flutter.

Mainly solitary, Lesser Spotted Woodpeckers resemble large Treecreepers as they move quietly up tree trunks and along the underside of branches.

69

Barn Swallow *Hirundo rustica*

Occurrence: April–October

Habitats: Almost anywhere; gathers at coastal marshes and reedbeds in autumn

Garden ranking: RARE

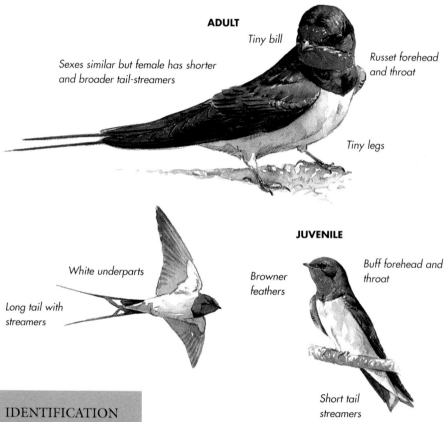

ADULT

Tiny bill

Sexes similar but female has shorter and broader tail-streamers

Russet forehead and throat

Tiny legs

JUVENILE

White underparts

Browner feathers

Buff forehead and throat

Long tail with streamers

Short tail streamers

IDENTIFICATION POINTS

- Long tail streamers
- Red face
- Pale underside
- Busy, chattering song
- Appears dark blue and white

CONFUSION SPECIES AND IDENTIFICATION NOTES

Most confusion is with flying birds. Swifts are larger, all brown and have sickle-shaped 'stiff' wings. House Martins are small with a white rump. Neither has the Swallow's long tail streamers or red facial markings.

LENGTH: 17–19 cm
WINGSPAN: 32–34.5 cm
VOICE: A busy, chattering song, similar to budgerigar; alarm call is a sharp 'flitt flitt'.
NESTBOX: Yes. Bowl nestbox.
NESTING: Both parents make nest-cup, almost exclusively on building beams and ledges. Mud is collected from the ground to bind the nest; if mud is unavailable, they will use the old nests of other birds. Nest revisited year after year. 4 or 5 red-speckled white eggs are laid between April–August.
FOOD & FEEDING: Flying insects mainly, but will take from foliage or the ground. Large flies such as bluebottles, as well as butterflies, bees and aphids.

Their graceful, seemingly effortless flight plus the russet throat with iridescent midnight-blue back make this a stunning bird. Unfortunately, good close-up views of Swallows in flight are difficult to get without the use of binoculars. They twist and turn, collecting insects which they store in a food ball in the throat; this handy feature allows them to catch the 6,000 insects a day each chick needs to survive.

It was once thought that Swallows buried themselves in muddy pools when they disappeared at the end of summer! This was perhaps due to their habit of collecting wet mud for their nests and collectively roosting in reedbeds before their departure to Africa.

Open, cup-shaped artificial nests are a great way to encourage this bird to breed in your garden.

House Martin *Delichon urbica*

Occurrence: April–September

Habitats: Almost anywhere, except very large cities. Lowland agricultural areas are especially popular. Absent northern Scotland.

Garden ranking: LESS COMMON

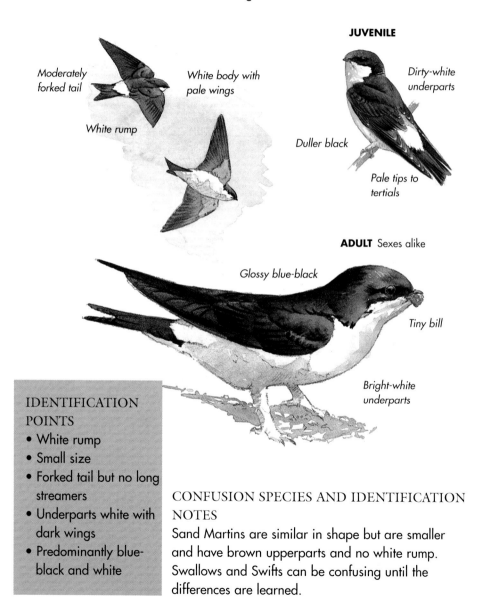

Moderately forked tail

White body with pale wings

JUVENILE

Dirty-white underparts

White rump

Duller black

Pale tips to tertials

ADULT Sexes alike

Glossy blue-black

Tiny bill

Bright-white underparts

IDENTIFICATION POINTS
- White rump
- Small size
- Forked tail but no long streamers
- Underparts white with dark wings
- Predominantly blue-black and white

CONFUSION SPECIES AND IDENTIFICATION NOTES

Sand Martins are similar in shape but are smaller and have brown upperparts and no white rump. Swallows and Swifts can be confusing until the differences are learned.

CHARACTERISTICS
LENGTH: 12.5–15 cm
WINGSPAN: 26–29 cm
VOICE: Noisiest at colonies. Song is chatty burst of chirps; call is a dry, repeated 'priit'.
NESTBOX: Yes. Bowl nestbox.
NESTING: Traditionally cliffs, but now buildings, especially eaves. A mud cup with entrance at the top. 2–5 white eggs laid between May–September. Both parents feed the young.
FOOD & FEEDING: Flying insects, but will sometimes take them from leaves or the ground. Greenfly, flies, beetles and ants.

These sociable birds like nesting in colonies as communal living offers safety in numbers. Young from earlier broods sometimes help their parents to feed their latest siblings. Cliffs were the traditional nest-sites for House Martins. Some still use them, but most nest on the eaves of buildings. They have been known to make nests on working ships and timber piles, and they will readily use a man-made bowl nestbox.

House Martins are gregarious birds, and will sometimes nest in close proximity to other species, as here with House Sparrows – which have taken over an old martin nest.

Once a suitable house is found, they will revisit year after year, saving time by repairing nests rather than building afresh. Three broods can be managed in one summer. The practice of knocking down nests from houses is illegal in the breeding season under UK law; fitting a splashboard over windows or doors helps stop mess.

Grey Wagtail *Motacilla cinerea*

Occurrence: All year round
Habitats: Near water in breeding season; at other times almost anywhere.
Garden ranking: RARE

MALE
Eye-stripe
Grey back
Black bib
White edges to wing feathers
Bright yellow underparts
Very long tail

JUVENILE
Pink lower mandible
White underparts
Bright yellow vent

FEMALE
White outer edge to tail
Pale grey throat
Paler yellow chest
Brown-pink legs

IDENTIFICATION POINTS
• Long wagging tail
• Grey head and back
• Yellow underparts

CONFUSION SPECIES AND IDENTIFICATION NOTES
Often confused with Yellow Wagtail (rare in gardens) – but the Grey Wagtail always has a grey back.

CHARACTERISTICS
LENGTH: 18–19 cm
WINGSPAN: 25–27 cm
VOICE: Call similar to Pied Wagtail, but higher-pitch 'tzee-tit'. Song is a short melodious burst of 'ziss-ziss-ziss'.
NESTBOX: Yes, open-fronted box.
NESTING: Both parents build a moss and grass nest lined with hair, always near water, usually in crevice or hole in banks and stone walls. 4–6 eggs, light brown with darker flecks, laid between late March–August. Will sometimes use old Dippers' nests.
FOOD & FEEDING: Insects, larvae, water snails, spiders, shrimps and tadpoles. Will feed in and next to water; also snatches insects in the air.

These birds can make an appearance almost anywhere. In the breeding season they hug the water's edge, while at other times they occur on the top of high-rise buildings, foraging on silage piles or strutting across lawns. They also love sewage works, probably due to the flies there. Many hill walkers following fast-flowing streams are familiar with this bird as it works the river, finding insects between rocks and water vegetation.

Of the four European wagtail species, the Grey wags its tail the most, running along, stopping suddenly but always pumping its long tail up and down. It will often fly up to grab a fly, land and continue to tail-wag. As the winter approaches Grey Wagtails tend to leave high ground and head lower down in search of food. Even so, many die in harsh winters.

During courtship the male (on the right) puts on an impressive display. He flies from perch to perch, fans his tail and puffs up his plumage.

Pied and White Wagtails
Motacilla alba yarrelli and *M. a. alba*

Occurrence: All year round
Habitats: Almost anywhere, especially parks, gardens and open farmland
Garden ranking: UNCOMMON

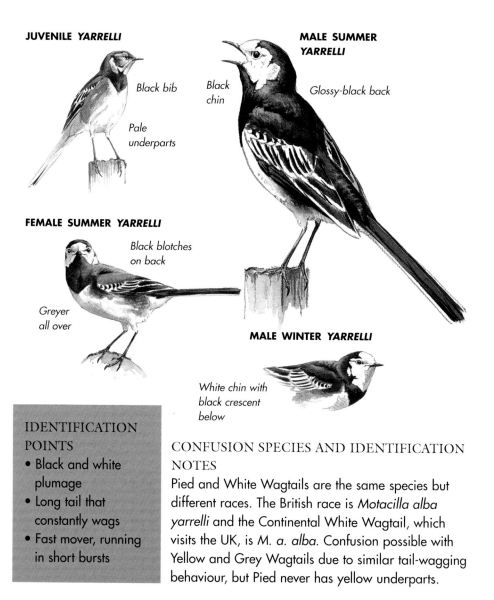

JUVENILE YARRELLI

Black bib

Pale underparts

MALE SUMMER YARRELLI

Black chin

Glossy-black back

FEMALE SUMMER YARRELLI

Black blotches on back

Greyer all over

MALE WINTER YARRELLI

White chin with black crescent below

IDENTIFICATION POINTS
- Black and white plumage
- Long tail that constantly wags
- Fast mover, running in short bursts

CONFUSION SPECIES AND IDENTIFICATION NOTES

Pied and White Wagtails are the same species but different races. The British race is *Motacilla alba yarrelli* and the Continental White Wagtail, which visits the UK, is *M. a. alba*. Confusion possible with Yellow and Grey Wagtails due to similar tail-wagging behaviour, but Pied never has yellow underparts.

CHARACTERISTICS
LENGTH: 16–18 cm
WINGSPAN: 25–30 cm
VOICE: Call is a short, sharp, loud 'chissick chissick'. Also loud, animated defence calls, 'chee-twee'. Song is a rather feeble twittering.
NESTBOX: Yes. Bird-shelf in foliage or open nestbox.
NESTING: Both parents build the nest, brood and rear chicks. 3–8 off-white eggs with brown/grey speckles laid between April–August. Nest of grass and moss, usually in nooks and crannies in wall or bank; sometimes old Blackbird nests are used.
FOOD & FEEDING: Main food is small insects, especially flies and midges. Will also take worms and seeds. Will pick up bits from under bird-table.

Although it likes wet habitats, you are just as likely to see this bird in town centres or open farmland. It spends a lot of the day searching for its main food – insects, and is often seen in car parks, where the flat, open ground makes food easier to see. Pied/White Wagtails are very territorial and will defend their patch against others. However, some will tolerate a younger male, but if food gets short, the adult male will soon chase him away.

In winter, Pied Wagtails will roost communally in incredibly large numbers, using reedbeds, city centres and even aircraft hangers. The largest recorded roost held around 5000 birds.

The male alba form or White Wagtail can be told from the yarrelli or Pied by its pale grey back and rump.

Waxwing *Bombycilla garrulus*

Occurrence: Winter visitor to UK, October–March
Habitats: Anywhere with berry-laden trees or shrubs
Rarity rating: RARE

Sexes similar, but female lacks strong yellow or red colours and black bib is smaller

ADULT

Also lighter colour, more graceful and slimmer profile

Black eye-mask and bib, plus obvious crest

Flight similar to Starling but has shorter tail

Grey rump

Yellow, white and red waxy tips to primaries

No red or yellow on wings

Orange-brown vent

Yellow tip to tail

JUVENILE

Less yellow on tail band

IDENTIFICATION POINTS

- Stocky, Starling-sized bird
- Prominent crest
- Usually in noisy feeding groups
- Often seen gorging on berries

CONFUSION SPECIES AND IDENTIFICATION NOTES

Can be confused with Starlings in flight. Waxwing has slightly shorter, stubby tail and broader wings.

CHARACTERISTICS
LENGTH: 18–21 cm
WINGSPAN: 32–35.5 cm
VOICE: Noisy in groups. Call is a whistling 'ssirrrrr', like a bell. Song is a mixture of call notes and raucous sounds.
NESTBOX: No.
NESTING: As a winter visitor to UK they don't nest here. Breeds in northern Scandinavia and Siberia in dense, mature pine forests. Both parents build a bowl-nest made of twigs and moss. Female incubates the 5–6 eggs; both feed young.
FOOD & FEEDING: Berries in winter, especially rowan, hawthorn, whitebeam and guelder rose. Also takes insects, but mainly in summer; these are caught on the wing with great agility.

When you see a group of birdwatchers standing in a supermarket car park peering up at a berry-laden tree, this means that Waxwings have arrived! A noisy, excitable flock of these exotic-looking birds always draws the crowds.

Although regular visitors, some years see huge numbers arriving in the UK – an event known as an irruption. In one such winter some 11,000 Waxwings were recorded in the UK, but such numbers are abnormal. Irruptions occur when the food crop fails in Scandinavia, forcing the birds to search further afield.

They get their name from the red waxy-looking tips to the secondary feathers. A good way to attract Waxwings to your garden is to plant winter berry-bearing shrubs, such as cotoneaster, pyracanthus, roses and rowan.

Waxwings have to eat around three times their own body weight each day to survive, so no berry bush is safe once they descend.

Wren *Troglodytes troglodytes*

Occurrence: All year round
Habitats: Woodland, dense undergrowth, gardens and parks
Garden ranking: VERY COMMON

ADULT
Sexes alike

Barred tail

Cream supercilium

Tail often cocked

Black eye-stripe

Long, thin bill

This tiny bird can burst into an incredibly loud trilling song.

IDENTIFICATION POINTS
- Tiny, brown-barred bird
- Tail often raised
- Scolding call
- Likes to flick around in dense undergrowth

CONFUSION SPECIES AND IDENTIFICATION NOTES
There's nothing like a Wren (except for a mouse), when it scurries out from the undergrowth and then runs back in. Calls can be confused with Robin's.

LENGTH: 9–10 cm
WINGSPAN: 13–17 cm
VOICE: Call a harsh, incredibly loud dry rattling 'tic-tic-tic'. Loud, explosive song; bursts of shrill and harsh (yet clear) warbling notes.
NESTBOX: Yes; special Wren balls, or open-fronted or tit-boxes, and even old tin watering cans!
NESTING: Male builds more than one ball-shaped nest of moss and grass, lined with feathers with side entrance. Attracts females by singing loudly near nest. Female lays 5–7 white and faintly speckled eggs between April–July.
FOOD & FEEDING: Mainly insects and spiders, but will dabble next to water to pick up tadpoles and aquatic insects. Will visit bird-table to remove small crumbs, grated cheese etc.

A walk in a British woodland is not complete without the trilling song of a Wren, or the loud ticking call it belts out when alarmed. Wrens are essentially woodland birds, but gardens have become welcome homes, especially if they have hedges and dense undergrowth. Although quite shy, Wrens will come out to investigate unusual noises.

The male Wren is busy at the start of the breeding season, and may make up to eight nests for the female to choose from. He may have two mates nesting in his territory, which can help boost numbers after harsh winters. Cold weather can cause up to 80 per cent mortality among Wrens; as Britain's second smallest bird (after the Goldcrest), they lose heat quickly in freezing conditions.

The Wren's small size can make surviving long periods of freezing weather very difficult. They will often huddle together to keep warm: 63 Wrens have been found in a single nest-box and about 100 were once recorded in an attic.

Dunnock *Prunella modularis*

Occurrence: All year round
Habitats: Almost anywhere with scrubby cover – gardens, parks, heathland
and even reedbeds in winter
Garden ranking: VERY COMMON

ADULT
Sexes alike, although the male
has more grey on his head

Thin, warbler-
like bill

Rich brown with
black streaks

Blue-grey face
with brown
cheeks

Males like to sing from
good vantage points; a
gate-post, top of a bush
or even a mole hill

Lacks grey

Boldly streaked
all over

JUVENILE

Pale chin

IDENTIFICATION
POINTS
- Sparrow-like markings
- Blue-grey head
- Slightly less round
  than House Sparrow
- Shuffling hops on the
  ground

CONFUSION SPECIES AND IDENTIFICATION
NOTES
Female House Sparrow. However, the Dunnock's
heavy streaks, grey head and thin bill makes it quite
different. Dunnocks are accentors and not members
of the sparrow family.

CHARACTERISTICS
LENGTH: 13–14.5 cm
WINGSPAN: 19–21 cm
VOICE: Alarm call is a strong piping 'tihh'; other calls are thinner, feebler. Song a rich, melodic patchwork of notes, similar to Wren but less aggressive.
NESTBOX: No.
NESTING: Female builds a moss and twig cup-nest. 4–5 blue eggs laid between April–August.
FOOD & FEEDING: Predominantly a ground feeder, taking a variety of insects and spiders. Will take fruit, berries and scraps that fall from the bird-table and feeders. Rarely sits on the bird-table.

The saying 'the quiet ones are usually the worse' fits the Dunnock well. It has a very complex sex life, practising polygyny, polyandry and polygynandry; i.e. one male with several females, one female with several males and several males with several females.

Dunnock display: this is usually performed on the ground, and males put on a curious wing flick to entice the female.

The female aims to secure as many mates as she can, as a mate will help feed young. The male aims to spread his genes as widely as possible, and will even cause his mate to eject another male's sperm by gently pecking her cloaca.

All of this results in many fights, and whilst courtship displays can involve up to eight birds, three is more common. Displaying birds gather in one spot, lifting and flicking one or both wings at a time.

Robin *Erithacus rubecula*

Occurrence: All year round, with migrants arriving in autumn
Habitats: Gardens, scrubby cover, parks, woods etc
Garden ranking: VERY COMMON

ADULT *Sexes alike; rusty red face and breast*

Brown back and tail

Grey fringe to breast

In cold weather, Robins puff out their feathers to trap warm air beneath. This can make them look twice their size

JUVENILE

Scaly-looking upperparts

Spotted breast

IDENTIFICATION POINTS
• Red breast
• Sweet, liquid song
• Brown back
• Sits in hunched pose

CONFUSION SPECIES AND IDENTIFICATION NOTES
The much smaller Red-breasted Flycatcher (rare in Britain) or possibly Common Redstart and Nightingale in poor light. Call can sometimes be confused with Wren's.

CHARACTERISTICS

LENGTH: 14 cm

WINGSPAN: 20–22 cm

VOICE: Alarm call is an urgent 'tic, tic, tic'. Song is a sweet, liquid, rambling warble.

NESTBOX: Yes, open-fronted.

NESTING: Female builds nest in well-hidden place, usually low to the ground. Ledges and crevices are also used. 5 or 6 bluish-white eggs with red flecks, laid between April–July. Both parents feed young; male becomes sole feeder if female nests again.

FOOD & FEEDING: Chief food is insects such as flies and beetles, but will eat worms, spiders, seeds and fruit in winter. Will collect scraps from bird-table and will take food from the hand, especially mealworms.

Robins can be very tame and may live up to 10 years, staying close to where they were born. Humans can strike up surprisingly close relationships with them, and in a cat-free garden Robins will feel safe enough to badger familiar gardeners for food, even hopping onto shoulders and feet. They will even take food from your hand, although taming garden Robins is not a good idea if cats are around. Large numbers of young Robins are killed by cats each year.

Territories are defended at all times, except when moulting.

Some Robins are travellers, and ringed birds have been recovered hundreds of miles away from their birthplace. In autumn, our native British Robins are joined by new arrivals from northern Europe. This can result in extra Robins at your bird-table.

Blackbird *Turdus merula*

Occurrence: All year round
Habitats: Almost everywhere – gardens, woodlands, parks, farms, scrub
Garden ranking: VERY COMMON

ADULT MALE

Yellow eye-ring

Yellow-orange bill

Wings often drooped

Fairly long tail

Often confused with female, but is streaked on upper- and underparts and usually more golden brown

JUVENILE

ADULT FEMALE

Darker bill

Paler throat

Chocolate brown

Streaked breast

MALE 1ST WINTER

No yellow eye-ring

Dark bill

IDENTIFICATION POINTS

- Male all black with yellow bill
- Female chocolate brown with paler bill
- Long tail often jerked upwards
- 'Pink-pink' alarm calls

CONFUSION SPECIES AND IDENTIFICATION NOTES

Male Blackbirds are quite unmistakable, although from a distance Starlings can look similar. Look out for the Starling's jerky walk. A pale, heavily-streaked female Blackbird could be confused with a Song Thrush. The rarer male Ring Ouzel looks like a male Blackbird but has a white crescent on breast.

CHARACTERISTICS
LENGTH: 24–25 cm
WINGSPAN: 34–38.5 cm
VOICE: Alarm or going-to-roost call is a harsh, metallic screeching 'pink-pink-pink'. The song is a beautiful yodelling, flutey, melodic tune with chuckles and warbles, and with pauses between the distinct phrases.
NESTBOX: Yes. Bird-shelf or open-fronted.
NESTING: Female builds nest, male helps collect vegetation. Cup-shaped, mud-lined and solid. 3–5 green-blue eggs with brown flecks, laid between late February–June. Both parents rear young. Can have up to five broods per year; sometimes reuses same nest.
FOOD & FEEDING: Wide-ranging diet from berries, worms, insects to tadpoles, small fish and snails. Will take almost anything from the bird-table, and adults bring fledglings to the table to encourage feeding. Be careful, however, not to offer them large-sized cat or dog biscuits: these swell in the stomach and can get stuck, causing birds to choke.

Watching the resident Blackbirds in your garden can be enormously rewarding. Close bonds can be formed with these birds. They can become very trusting, and will bring their whole family to feed at your bird-table, giving spectacular views. They will hop around your feet, and may even pop into your house.

Don't be alarmed if you see a Blackbird spread-eagled on the ground with gaping mouth: just like us, they love to sun-bathe.

Blackbirds are prolific breeders, having up to five broods per year, and could turn your garden into a nursery for up to 20 birds during the breeding season. They may start breeding as early as February if the weather is mild. Although most of our garden Blackbirds are resident, during the winter we play host to many northern European birds, who abandon their breeding sites to escape severe weather.

Fieldfare *Turdus pilaris*

Occurrence: Winter visitor, September–April/May
Habitats: Fields, gardens, parks, hedges. A few breed in Scotland
Garden ranking: RARE

ADULT *Sexes alike*

Strong bill

Grey head, pale
supercilium

Chestnut back

Yellowish throat,
ochre breast with
brown flecks

Grey rump
obvious

JUVENILE

Pale-grey back

Long, dark
tail

White under-
wings

Pale supercilium
wing coverts,
pale spots

IDENTIFICATION POINTS

- Large stocky thrush
- Strongly contrasting colours
- 'Chak-chak' call in flight

CONFUSION SPECIES AND IDENTIFICATION NOTES

All thrushes can be confusing for novice bird-watchers. Song Thrushes and Redwings are much smaller. Mistle Thrushes are slightly larger than Fieldfares and lack their contrast and colours.

CHARACTERISTICS
LENGTH: 25.5–27 cm
WINGSPAN: 39–42 cm
VOICE: Call is a loud 'chacker-chak-chak; a thin nasal 'seee' is often uttered in flight. Song is a tuneless, sqeaky warble and not often heard in Britain.
NESTBOX: No.
NESTING: Female builds a cup-shaped nest with twigs and bound with mud. Both parents feed young. 5–6 glossy pale-blue eggs with brick-red flecks, laid between April–July.
FOOD & FEEDING: A wide variety, from insects, spiders, worms to berries such as rowan, juniper, hawthorn and holly. Also orchard windfalls.

These large and tough northern birds are not to be messed with while at the nest. They see off any intruder, including humans, with noisy alarm calls, dive-bombing and even excrement, unleashed with precision. A few pairs breed in Scotland, while most prefer the cooler northern European climate, particularly Scandinavia and northern Russia.

As winter approaches, many Fieldfares move south to escape the harsh weather. Thousands reach the UK, where large winter flocks are a common sight, feeding in open fields and frequently joining forces with other visiting thrushes, such as Redwings. During our severest winters, when the hedges have been stripped of berries, Fieldfares will come into gardens in a desperate search for food. They are very partial to apples left on the ground.

The Fieldfare's strong bill enables it to push aside snow or detritus to find food. Leaving windfall fruit will encourage their visits.

Song Thrush *Turdus philomelos*

Occurrence: All year round, with migrants arriving in autumn
Habitats: Gardens, parks, woodlands and hedgerows
Garden ranking: LESS COMMON

ADULT *Sexes alike*

Warm-brown
upperparts

Arrow-head spots
falling in loosely formed
lines on underside

Buff-yellow flanks
and breast

Pale legs

Rusty-buff
underwing

Fairly short
tail

Pale buff streaks
on upperparts

JUVENILE

IDENTIFICATION
POINTS
• Breast spots fall in
  loose lines
• Spectacular song
• Warm-brown
  upperparts
• Smaller than blackbird
• Rusty-buff underwing
  in flight

CONFUSION SPECIES AND IDENTIFICATION
NOTES
All thrushes can be confusing at first. Redwings look
similar but have a cream supercilium, red flanks and
are slightly smaller. Mistle Thrushes are much larger,
with grey-brown upperparts and heavy black breast-
spots, splattered unevenly over their underparts. They
also lack the 'kind' expression of the Song Thrush.

CHARACTERISTICS
LENGTH: 20–23 cm
WINGSPAN: 33–36cm cm
VOICE: Alarm call is a scolding 'chuk-chuk'; other calls sharp 'zit'. Song is a beautiful, languid fluty song, easy to remember as it repeats notes three or four times. Includes mimicry in its repertoire.
NESTBOX: No.
NESTING: Cup-shaped, mud-lined nest with grasses and twigs made by female. 3–5 pale blue, black-spotted eggs laid between March–July. Nest reused for later broods. Nest usually low down, in a tree or shrub near to trunk.
FOOD & FEEDING: Famous for its snail-smashing technique, but also eats worms, fruit and berries. Reluctant to sit on bird-table, but will feed from below, taking a variety of scraps. Sultanas are a real favourite.

Harsh winters can seriously affect the Song Thrush, but other factors have helped cause a 53 per cent decline in the last 20 years. Basically, there is not enough food for young thrushes to survive their first year, probably due to intensive farming methods.

Incentives to encourage 'wildlife-friendly' farming, plus reduced slug pellet use by gardeners, might help Song Thrushes. Meanwhile, in 2005 the species dropped out of the top 20 commonest birds in the RSPB's *Big Garden Birdwatch* survey for the first time.

Their gorgeous song is similar to a Blackbird's with repeated phrases, and many a novice birdwatcher has mistaken it for a Nightingale. The second part of the scientific name philomelos is Greek for 'song-lover'.

The delicate blue and black speckled pattern of the Song Thrush's eggs is distinctive. A pair may have as many as four broods of young in one year.

91

Redwing *Turdus iliacus*

Occurrence: Mainly winter visitor, October–March
Habitats: Open fields, large gardens and mixed woodland
Garden ranking: RARE

ADULT *Sexes alike*

Bold cream supercilium

Dark eye-stripe

Rusty red flanks

Black tip to
yellow bill

Cream sub-
moustachial stripe

Heavily streaked
underparts

JUVENILE

Buff spots
on back

Slightly pointed wings

Rusty-red
underwing

Strong head
pattern

Pale tips to
some wing
feathers

IDENTIFICATION
POINTS
- Smallest thrush in UK
- Strong cream
  supercilium
- Red flanks

CONFUSION SPECIES AND IDENTIFICATION
NOTES
Song Thrushes look similar, but Redwing always
shows a bold, creamy-white supercilium. Even if the
red flanks aren't visible, the supercilium will be. In
flight the rusty-red underwings are darker than Song
Thrush's.

LENGTH: 19–23 cm
WINGSPAN: 33–34.5 cm
VOICE: Alarm call is a scolding 'tret-tret-tret'. Call during migration is a drawn-out 'seeip'. Song (rarely heard in Britain) is usually in two parts: jumbled flutey notes, then deeper low twittering.
NESTBOX: No.
NESTING: Rare breeder in Scotland and northern England. Breeds in northern European birch forests. Female builds cup nest of moss, dry grass and mud, low to or on ground. Both parents feed young. 4–6 speckled green-blue eggs laid between April–June.
FOOD & FEEDING: Winter food consists of fruits and berries. In summer, takes insects, worms, slugs. Harsh winters see many Redwings visiting gardens to raid berry bushes and windfall apples.

Planting shrubs with winter berries, such as hawthorn, cotoneaster and pyracanthus, may entice Redwings to visit your garden in winter. Severe weather forces them into gardens, even onto the bird-table if fruit is on offer.

The UK's smallest thrush starts to arrive in October; some winters see nearly a million birds visiting Britain. Berry-laden hedges and worm-filled grassland help them to survive the winter. But when the bushes have been stripped and the fields are snow-covered, then these birds may need our help. As temperatures drop, this small thrush seeks the warmth and cover of gardens and woodlands to survive. Clearing snow and putting out apples, pears, dried fruit, potatoes, and even grated cheese, will all increase their chances of survival.

Redwings are highly gregarious, feeding and roosting with other thrushes, especially Fieldfares. Scandinavian Redwings arrive along the east coast, while the larger, darker Icelandic race visit our western coast, and may move further south to Spain and northern Africa.

Mistle Thrush *Turdus viscivorus*

Occurrence: All year round. Migrants in Autumn
Habitats: Almost anywhere – farmland, gardens and woodlands
Garden ranking: RARE

White underwing

ADULT *Sexes alike*

White eye-ring

Pale cheek-patch

Grey-brown back

Strong, direct flight

Heavy random dark spots on underparts

White marks on back and head

Paler rump

Lacks obvious cheek- patch

JUVENILE

IDENTIFICATION POINTS
- Largest thrush
- Heavily spotted underparts
- Grey-brown back
- Often stands to attention

CONFUSION SPECIES AND IDENTIFICATION NOTES

Commonly confused with the Song Thrush, a much warmer brown, 'kinder-looking', bird. The Mistle Thrush is larger, cold-looking and grey brown, with an upright, aggressive 'ready to fight' stance. The half-moon spots on the Mistle Thrush are splattered all over, whereas the Song Thrush's arrow-head spots fall in loose lines down breast. Redwings are smaller and browner with a cream supercilium.

CHARACTERISTICS
LENGTH: 26–29 cm
WINGSPAN: 42–47.5 cm
VOICE: Alarm call is a hard, dry rattle. Song similar to Blackbird but less fluty.
NESTBOX: No.
NESTING: Female builds cup-shaped nest of roots, grasses, fleece and moss
cemented with mud, usually in fork of tree a fair distance from ground. 3–6 eggs
laid February–July. Eggs variable in colour, pinkish cream with brown blotches
or pale green-blue with darker flecks.
FOOD & FEEDING: Insects, berries and fruit. In winter they will fiercely defend
fruiting bushes. Will visit bird-tables and take a variety of foods, especially fruit.
May become territorial, chasing off any other birds that dare land on the table.

This hardy brute of a thrush is quite a charming character. Its habit of belting out its song in rainy, grey weather earned it the nickname 'storm-cock'. Thomas Hardy, hearing it on such a day, was amazed that such a cheery song could be heard in such bad conditions, and as a result was inspired to write his poem *The Darkling Thrush*.

Once a good food source is found, the Mistle Thrush will defend it fiercely. The smaller members of the thrush family, like the Redwing and Song Thrush, are no match for this bird.

Aggressive when defending its nest or food supply, it can chase off cats, dogs and even humans if they get too close. Its threatening attacks with rapid alarm calls and dive-bombing flights, which may include actual strikes to the head, terrifies anything on the receiving end. The name 'Mistle' refers to its fondness for mistletoe berries, although in some areas it is also known as the 'holly thrush'.

Blackcap *Sylvia atricapilla*

Occurrence: April–October, but some overwinter in gardens
Habitats: Hedgerows, woodland with dense undergrowth, gardens and parks
Absent from northern Scotland and most of western Ireland.
Garden ranking: UNCOMMON

Black cap

ADULT MALE

Grey-brown upperparts

Pale-grey underparts

ADULT FEMALE

Red-brown cap

MALE 1ST WINTER

Pale-brown underparts

Cap a mixture of red-brown and black

Grey legs

IDENTIFICATION POINTS	CONFUSION SPECIES AND IDENTIFICATION NOTES
• Sparrow-sized grey-brown warbler • Male has black cap • Female has brown cap	Garden Warblers share similar habitats and behaviour, but lack the coloured cap and contrasting markings. Marsh and Willow Tits also have black caps but are much smaller, with black bibs and bright white cheeks.

CHARACTERISTICS
LENGTH: 13–15 cm
WINGSPAN: 20–23 cm
VOICE: Alarm call sounds just like two stones striking each other. Beautiful, rich warbling song, similar to Garden Warbler but more manic, with shorter phrases and sudden outbursts.
NESTBOX: No.
NESTING: Male half-builds several delicate cup nests in dense foliage low to the ground; female chooses one for completion. 4–6 pale-brown-spotted eggs laid between April–June.
FOOD & FEEDING: A wide range of food is taken: insects such as caterpillars, flies and beetles in summer, switching to fruit and berries in winter.

England is now a firm favourite holiday destination for the Blackcap in winter. It's heartening to see that some bird species are actually increasing in numbers, and the Blackcap is one of these. Since the 1970s their numbers have been on the up, so seeing them in winter is an increasingly regular experience.

Our breeding birds leave at the end of summer, heading for the warmth of Mediterranean Spain, Portugal and North Africa. Birds from west-central Europe leave their breeding grounds to escape the winter and many end up in England, where milder winters and plentiful bird-tables help them to survive. One of the earliest warblers to arrive, they are also called the 'March Nightingale', and often puff out their throat feathers and slightly raise their black caps while singing.

Blackcaps are much more confident birds than Garden Warblers, and those visiting bird-tables may even chase off other feeding birds.

Easier to see than Garden Warblers, Blackcaps like to sing from high vantage point in shrubs.

Garden Warbler *Sylvia borin*

Occurrence: April–September (passage migrants in October)
Habitats: Woodland scrub, dense undergrowth and hedgerows. Absent from northern Scotland
Garden ranking: RARE

Hint of a pale supercilium

Grey neck-side

Grey bill

ADULT *Sexes alike*

'Kind' expression

Greyish legs

JUVENILE

Similar to adult but colours appear fresher and can look more olive green

IDENTIFICATION POINTS

- No distinctive markings/very plain
- Great Tit-sized warbler
- Grey-brown plumage
- 'Kind' expression

CONFUSION SPECIES AND IDENTIFICATION NOTES

For novice birdwatchers, identifying warblers is just as difficult as non-breeding waders! Chiffchaffs and Willow Warblers are smaller and have more colour (green). The shy, skulking behaviour of the Garden Warbler is similar to that of the Blackcap, but the latter's black or brown cap separates the two species. The Reed Warbler has a much larger bill, is usually in different habitat, and is brighter and more russet.

CHARACTERISTICS

LENGTH: 13–14 cm

WINGSPAN: 20–24.5 cm

VOICE: Alarm call 'chek-chek-chek', getting faster as more agitated. Also a low 'churrr'. Beautiful trickling song, more mellow than Blackcap, with less interruptions and longer phrases.

NESTBOX: No.

NESTING: Male half-builds several 'cock nests', the female choosing one for completion. Cup-shaped, of dry grass, leaves and plant stems, and usually low in bush. 4–5 white or buff speckled eggs laid between May–July.

FOOD & FEEDING: Mainly insects, but switches to fruit (figs on migration) and berries in the winter. Very rare visitor to bird-table, tends to look on from the safety of nearby bushes, making a quick dash to grab small bits of fruit and cheese.

What this bird lacks in colour it certainly makes up for in song. This shy, plain-looking warbler sits deep in a bush and sings a beautiful song which would rival any Nightingale. Its calm demeanour means that when it is finally spotted it rarely seems to panic. It doesn't dart off quickly, or flick its tail, but just calmly goes about its business. Even the song is more laid back than the Blackcap's.

Its facial expression reinforces its character; the kind-looking dark eyes giving a gentle appearance. The name 'Garden' Warbler is rather misleading as it's really not a garden bird, preferring woodland. However, it will visit large gardens with woodland fringes and lots of dense-foliaged, tall trees with rich undergrowth.

Garden Warblers can be a nightmare to find in dense foliage. Even experienced birdwatchers may take some time trying to decide if it's a Blackcap or Garden Warbler, before it finally pops out at the top of the bush.

Chiffchaff *Phylloscopus collybita*

Occurrence: March–September, but some overwinter
Habitats: Anywhere with leafy trees; gardens and parks
Garden ranking: RARE

ADULT *Sexes alike*

Pale supercilium   Dark eye-stripe

Brownish-olive upperparts

Yellow tinge
on breast

Dirty-white
underparts

Dark legs

ADULT: *ABIETINUS* RACE
From Scandinavia, seen
in Britain during their
autumn migration.

JUVENILE

Browner upperparts

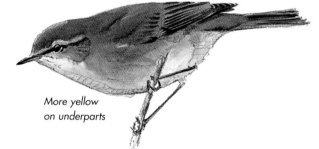

More yellow
on underparts

IDENTIFICATION POINTS

- Blue Tit-sized warbler
- Often seen flicking through leafy branches
- Darker legs than Willow Warbler
- Darker, greyer than Willow Warbler
- Familiar 'chiff-chaff' song

CONFUSION SPECIES AND IDENTIFICATION NOTES

Often confused with the Willow Warbler (until the very different song is heard). Chiffchaff has darker legs, shorter wings (they end as the tail begins); Willow Warbler is normally brighter coloured with more yellow and a more obvious supercilium.

LENGTH: 10–11 cm
WINGSPAN: 15–21 cm
VOICE: Call is a soft whistling 'huitt'. As the name suggests, the song is a sharp, monotonous 'chiff-chaff-chiff-chaff ', the 'chiff' being higher-pitched than the 'chaff'.
NESTBOX: No.
NESTING: Female builds a ball-shaped nest with side entrance, just above ground level and hidden in dense foliage i.e. grass or bramble. 6–7 white eggs with pale purple-brown flecks, laid between April–July.
FOOD & FEEDING: Mainly insects, especially midges, flies and aphids. Will occasionally take seeds.

Spring has arrived when you hear the familiar 'chiff-chaff' song one sunny morning in March. With the recent string of mild winters in Britain, Chiffchaffs are singing earlier and earlier. No one is sure if some of our breeding birds are now overwintering or if other European birds come here, but more Chiffchaffs are certainly spending the winter in the UK.

This tiny bird, about the size of a Blue Tit, covers many miles on its annual migration to Africa. Until recently it was thought that British Chiffchaffs spent the winter in the Mediterranean, but ringing has shown that they fly further south, over the Western Sahara to Mauritania or even as far as Guinea-Bissau. A remarkable journey for such a small bird!

These 'leaf warblers' are often seen busily collecting insects from the underside of leaves. They also make quick horizontal dashes, snatching insects from the air.

Willow Warbler *Phylloscopus trochilus*

Occurrence: April–September
Habitats: Anywhere with young trees; woodland edge, scrub, gardens
Garden ranking: RARE

ADULT *Sexes alike*

Longer primary length than Chiffchaff

Yellow supercilium

Pale yellow tinge to underparts

Pale belly

Pale legs

JUVENILE

Yellow-brown back

Dark eye-stripe

Yellower underparts than adult

Grey back

White underparts

White supercilium

NORTHERN RACE ACREDULA

IDENTIFICATION POINTS

- Blue Tit-sized warbler
- Yellowish plumage
- Yellow supercilium
- Pale legs
- Longer wings than Chiffchaff

CONFUSION SPECIES AND IDENTIFICATION NOTES

The Chiffchaff's similar size and plumage can confuse even experienced birdwatchers. Willow Warblers are usually more yellow, with paler underparts, but this can be less apparent in bad light. They have paler legs than Chiffchaff and longer primaries. However, the two species' songs are very different. The scarcer Wood Warbler also looks quite similar, but is rarely a garden bird.

CHARACTERISTICS
LENGTH: 10.5–11.5 cm
WINGSPAN: 16.5–22 cm
VOICE: Call is similar to Chiffchaff's soft 'huit', but with more emphasis on the 'hu'. Song is a fast and effortless cascade of descending clear notes.
NESTBOX: No.
NESTING: Ball-shaped nest of moss and grass with side entrance, close to or on the ground. 6–7 eggs, cream with red blotches, laid between late April–July. Males can have more than one mate. Both parents feed young.
FOOD & FEEDING: Insects, particularly aphids, midges and spiders. Eats berries in late summer and autumn.

During courtship, the male chases the female, then lands next to her and starts to lift one or both wings. He also fans his tail and quivers all over until she submits.

'A bird that warbles in the willows' is a great way to describe the sweet, liquid song of the Willow Warbler, a familiar sound in boggy moorland bushes or forest edge. In July and August our Willow Warblers start to make their way south to spend the winter in Africa. Remarkably, this tiny 10g bundle of feathers reaches almost halfway down the west coast of Africa.

Unlike any other British bird, the Willow Warbler undergoes two complete moults each year: once in summer, and then again after their winter migration to Africa. Numbers in England have declined steadily over the last 25 years, while in Scotland they have remained stable. The decline could be due to wetter summers in England and/or to drought in Africa.

Goldcrest *Regulus regulus*

Occurrence: All year round (with an influx in autumn/winter)
Habitats: Coniferous or mixed woodland, churchyard yews, gardens,
deciduous trees with conifers nearby
Garden ranking: RARE

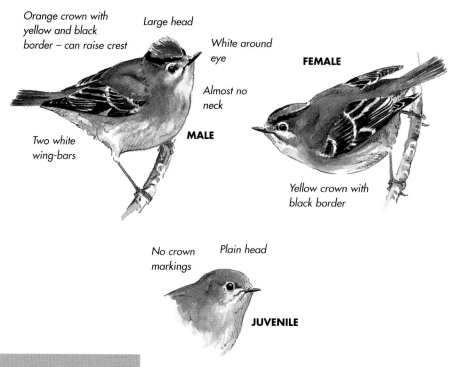

Orange crown with yellow and black border – can raise crest

Large head

White around eye

Almost no neck

Two white wing-bars

MALE

FEMALE

Yellow crown with black border

No crown markings

Plain head

JUVENILE

IDENTIFICATION POINTS
- Europe's smallest bird (with Firecrest)
- Yellow stripe on crown
- Busily flicks through trees
- High-pitched 'tsee' calls

CONFUSION SPECIES AND IDENTIFICATION NOTES

The rarer Firecrest looks similar but has a broad white supercilium.

Very rarely, Pallas's Warblers drop by in autumn on migration from Asia. They are similar, but have three clear yellow stripes on their darker crown.

CHARACTERISTICS
LENGTH: 8.5–9 cm
WINGSPAN: 13.5–15.5 cm
VOICE: Call is a high-pitched, whistling 'tsee-tsee-tsee'. Song is a high-pitched and rapidly-repeated 'see-sissisyu-see'.
NESTBOX: No.
NESTING: Deep, cup-shaped nest of moss, cobwebs and lichen, suspended like a hammock between conifer branches. 7–8 white, red-spotted eggs laid between April–June. Both birds build nest and feed young.
FOOD & FEEDING: Almost exclusively insects, but will eat small seeds. Occasionally investigates bird-tables, taking small crumbs and seeds.

Most of the Goldcrests in the UK are resident, rarely moving far away from where they were hatched. Northern European birds flee the cold winters where they breed, resulting in a considerable influx of Goldcrests to the UK each autumn. Europe's joint smallest bird (with Firecrest) is capable of flying from Scandinavia and Russia to Britain, a remarkable feat for something that only weighs 5–7g and is barely as long as your index finger!

Being so tiny, British Goldcrests suffer heavy losses during severe spells of cold weather and snow, but the hardier Scandinavian birds can survive low temperatures and there are records of birds overwintering in sub-zero temperatures in coastal northern Norway. The current trend of warmer UK winters should help bolster the British Goldcrest population.

Goldcrests are often seen busily flicking through foliage in search of insects. Their restless determination in the quest for food can mean great views as they distractedly pop out from cover.

Spotted Flycatcher *Muscicapa striata*

Occurrence: May–August. Migrating birds from northern Europe
can be seen in September.
Habitats: Open woodland, parkland and large gardens
Garden ranking: RARE

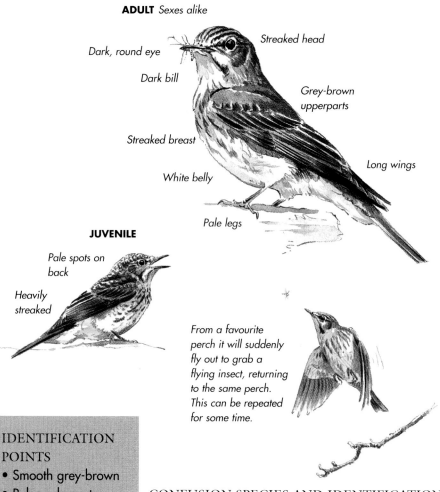

ADULT *Sexes alike*

Dark, round eye

Streaked head

Dark bill

Grey-brown
upperparts

Streaked breast

Long wings

White belly

JUVENILE

Pale legs

Pale spots on
back

Heavily
streaked

From a favourite
perch it will suddenly
fly out to grab a
flying insect, returning
to the same perch.
This can be repeated
for some time.

IDENTIFICATION
POINTS
• Smooth grey-brown
• Pale underparts
• Streaks on breast
• Quick, vertical flights
  to snatch insects

CONFUSION SPECIES AND IDENTIFICATION
NOTES
Other flycatchers such as immature and female Pied.
There are other flycatcher species in Europe, but only
the Pied and Spotted commonly visit the UK.

LENGTH: 13.5–14.5 cm
WINGSPAN: 23–25.5 cm
VOICE: Call is a shrill 'tzee. Alarm call: a dry, clicking 'tzek-tk-tk'. Song is composed of high-pitched, sqeaky notes, similar to a slow-turning wheel.
NESTBOX: Yes. Open fronted nestboxes or bird-shelf.
NESTING: Will nest almost anywhere in crevice, hole or ledge. Site needs to be very well hidden, with bushy plants growing against walls a favourite. 4–5 pale green-brown speckled eggs laid between May-June. Both parents feed young.
FOOD & FEEDING: Insects, mainly on the wing but bad weather will force them to feed from the ground and amongst foliage. Females eat snail shells and woodlice – the calcium helps egg production.

This once-common British visitor is declining so quickly in the UK that it is becoming an increasingly scarce sight. Between 1970–98 numbers fell by a worrying 78 per cent. The situation hasn't improved since, and the sight of a Spotted Flycatcher perched on a favourite branch waiting to snap up an insect is sadly no longer common. The decline is general and may be due to a problem in their African wintering home, perhaps drought.

The Spotted Flycatcher's distinctive flight pattern when hunting helps with identification at a distance. Sometimes it hovers briefly in front of foliage waiting for insect to emerge.

Not so much spotted as streaked, this flycatcher has fairly indistinguished plumage but is handsome and sleek, with fantastically acrobatic insect-hunting behaviour. If you are lucky enough to see these birds in your garden, put some open-fronted or shelf nestboxes in well-hidden places – and cross your fingers!

Long-tailed Tit *Aegithalos caudatus*

Occurrence: All year round
Habitats: Woodland, parks, gardens and hedgerows.
Garden ranking: LESS COMMON

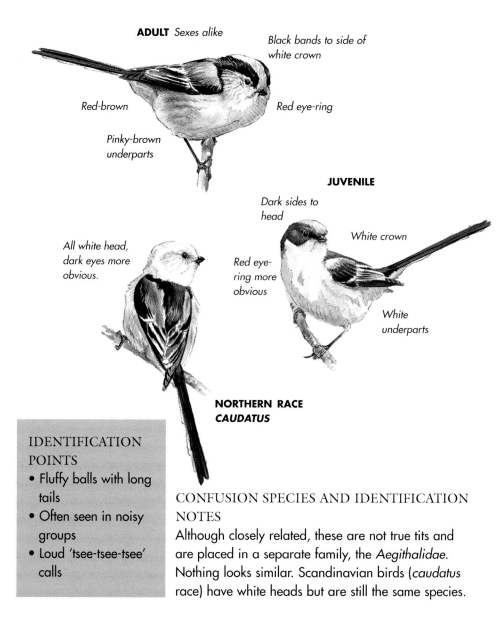

ADULT *Sexes alike*

Black bands to side of white crown

Red-brown

Red eye-ring

Pinky-brown underparts

JUVENILE

Dark sides to head

White crown

All white head, dark eyes more obvious.

Red eye-ring more obvious

White underparts

NORTHERN RACE
CAUDATUS

IDENTIFICATION POINTS
• Fluffy balls with long tails
• Often seen in noisy groups
• Loud 'tsee-tsee-tsee' calls

CONFUSION SPECIES AND IDENTIFICATION NOTES
Although closely related, these are not true tits and are placed in a separate family, the *Aegithalidae*. Nothing looks similar. Scandinavian birds (*caudatus* race) have white heads but are still the same species.

CHARACTERISTICS

LENGTH: 13–15 cm, of which 7–9 cm is tail

WINGSPAN: 16–19 cm

VOICE: Call is a piercing, high-pitched 'tsee-tsee-tsee', repeated rapidly by many birds in succession. Contact call is a softer 'thrup'. The soft, twittering song is seldom heard.

NESTBOX: No.

NESTING: A masterly-constructed oval nest with side entrance, made by both parents and placed in dense cover. Of moss, cobwebs and hair, lined with feathers and with lichen on the outside. Nest expands as chicks grow. 8–12 red-speckled white eggs laid between March–May. Both parents rear young, sometimes with help of flock members who have failed to breed.

FOOD & FEEDING: Main food is insects, especially spiders. Also pecks at lichens and algae. Visits windows to pick off insects and will also attack its own reflection! Regular bird-table visitor, especially in winter, preferring fatty scraps, peanuts and fat balls.

Nothing can compete with the Long-tailed Tit for acrobatic skills, entertainment, noise and all-round endearing qualities. You rarely see just one bird on your feeder, as they travel around in family groups of between 8–20 birds, noisily announcing their presence with their characteristic and excitable 'tsee-tsee-tsee' calls. Once a food source has been found, one or two birds may drop down first, constantly calling until, one by one, they fly from tree to tree until they all descend on the feeders.

Vulnerable in severe winters, they tend to have large broods, sometimes up to twelve chicks. Luckily, their cleverly-made nest has an elastic quality which means it can expand to fit all the family members. Parents have to bend their tails backwards over their heads to fit in the nest.

Due to their relatively large surface area and small body mass, heat loss can be devastating for Long-tailed Tits in cold winters. Because of this, communal roosting is a must for their survival.

Blue Tit *Cyanistes caeruleus*

Occurrence: All year round
Habitats: Woodland, hedgerows, parks and gardens
Garden ranking: VERY COMMON

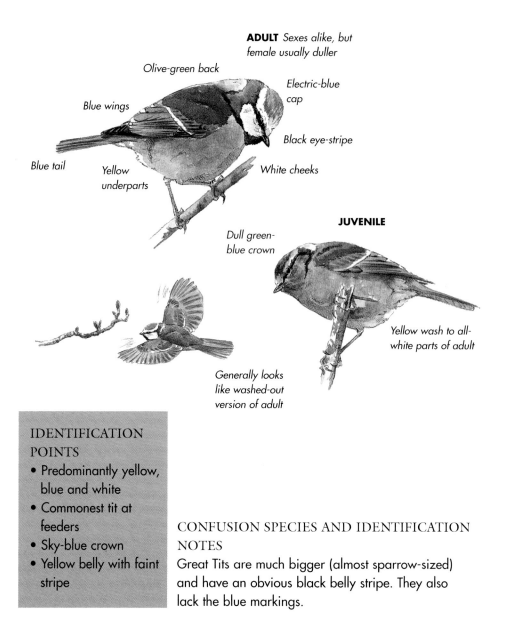

ADULT *Sexes alike, but female usually duller*

Olive-green back

Electric-blue cap

Blue wings

Black eye-stripe

Blue tail

Yellow underparts

White cheeks

JUVENILE

Dull green-blue crown

Yellow wash to all-white parts of adult

Generally looks like washed-out version of adult

IDENTIFICATION POINTS
- Predominantly yellow, blue and white
- Commonest tit at feeders
- Sky-blue crown
- Yellow belly with faint stripe

CONFUSION SPECIES AND IDENTIFICATION NOTES
Great Tits are much bigger (almost sparrow-sized) and have an obvious black belly stripe. They also lack the blue markings.

CHARACTERISTICS
LENGTH: 10.5–11.5 cm
WINGSPAN: 17.5–20 cm
VOICE: A variety of calls: a thin 'si-si-i-churrr', also 'ptsee-tsee-dee-dee'. Alarm
call is a 'churr-urr-urr'. Song is a clear continuous 'pseet-see-sirrrr'.
NESTBOX: Yes, frequently.
NESTING: Nests in hole or crevice in tree, lined with moss, grasses and soft
materials. 5–12 red-speckled white eggs laid between March–June. Eggs laid at
daily intervals, brooding starts when last egg is laid. Female builds nest, both
parents feed young.
FOOD & FEEDING: Mainly insects and spiders in summer, especially caterpillars
when feeding young. Other foods taken in winter include seeds, fruits and
berries. A keen and regular visitor to bird-tables and a variety of feeders.

The brightly coloured Blue Tit is a common bird-table
guest and it's worth buying bird food to attract these
lively birds alone. Although the Blue Tit weighs around
10g to the Great's 17g, their small size doesn't mean
they are a push-over – they will even take on the much
larger Great Tit if annoyed. Most of the squabbles at
feeders seem to be with their own species, however.
They constantly bicker amongst themselves, raising their
crests and dropping their wings in defiance. Their small
size and weight mean Blue Tits can feed from very thin
branches and foliage that
would not support the hefty
Great Tit. Whilst you may
only see a few at your
feeder at any one time, up
to 20 birds may actually
be visiting.

*During the nesting period,
parents are often seen leaving
the nest carrying small white
parcels in their bills. These are
piles of fledgling poo, which
the parents must remove to
keep the nest clean.*

*During courtship the male flies with very fast wing-beats then
lands on a branch. The female takes on a begging stance
(similar to juveniles begging for food), while shivering her
wings at the male.*

111

Great Tit *Parus major*

Occurrence: All year round
Habitats: A variety of woodland, parks, gardens and hedgerows
Garden ranking: VERY COMMON

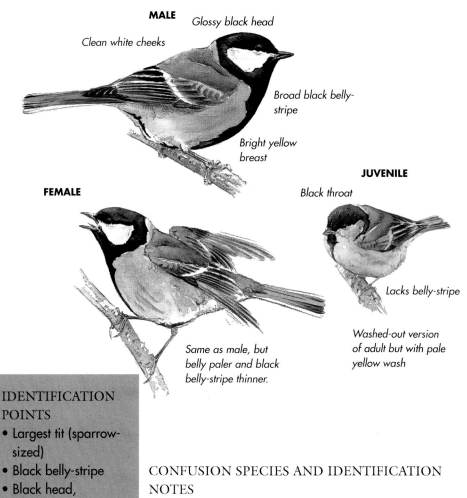

MALE
Glossy black head
Clean white cheeks
Broad black belly-stripe
Bright yellow breast

JUVENILE
Black throat
Lacks belly-stripe
Washed-out version of adult but with pale yellow wash

FEMALE
Same as male, but belly paler and black belly-stripe thinner.

IDENTIFICATION POINTS
- Largest tit (sparrow-sized)
- Black belly-stripe
- Black head, contrasting white cheeks
- Regular bird-table visitors

CONFUSION SPECIES AND IDENTIFICATION NOTES

Once you have worked out all the tits, identifying this big bruiser should be easy. Remember its size and the black belly-stripe. Juvenile Blue Tits are similar but juvenile Great Tits show darker head and have dark throat with beginnings of belly stripe.

112

CHARACTERISTICS
LENGTH: 13.5–14 cm
WINGSPAN: 22.5–25.5 cm
VOICE: Has a wide repertoire of calls, mainly cheerful and metallic, including see-sawing 'tea-cher, tea-cher, tea-cher' and 'pee-too, pee-too, pee-too'; also 'ping, ping'. Song is variation of loud, mechanical 'ti-ta, ti-ta, ti-ta'.
NESTBOX: Yes, regularly.
NESTING: Uses holes in wood or walls. Female makes nest and lines with moss, feathers, fur and hair. 5–12 red-brown-speckled white eggs laid between April–July. Both parents feed young in nest and up to two weeks after fledging.
FOOD & FEEDING: Mainly insects in summer, especially weevils and caterpillars for young. The large bill is capable of opening harder seeds and fruit in winter, such as hazelnuts and beechmast. A variety of food is taken at the table but peanuts seem to be a firm favourite.

This formidable tit has seen its numbers increase over the past forty years, no doubt helped by our efforts to feed and house them. Europe's largest member of the tit family has some less than endearing qualities. They bully their smaller relatives, as a short stint watching a bird-table will confirm. Blue Tits put up the best fight, but other small tits make a swift departure, not surprisingly considering that Great Tits can crack open hazelnuts with their powerful bills. There are reports of them killing and even eating other birds, including members of their own species. They can't be all bad though, as they frequently join up with other tits in large feeding flocks.

Although they dominate all other tits, as soon as a Nuthatch or Great Spotted Woodpecker arrives, Great Tits quickly back off.

Coal Tit *Periparus ater*

Occurrence: All year round
Habitats: Prefers coniferous woodland but also in deciduous, also in bushes, hedgerows, parks and gardens
Garden ranking: COMMON

ADULT *Sexes alike*

Distinctive white stripe on nape

Olive-brown back

Two white wing-bars

Black head white cheeks

JUVENILE

Duller appearance

Head browner, yellow wash to white cheeks and nape mark

Blue-grey upperparts

Whiter cheeks

Pale buff-pink underparts

NORTHERN EUROPEAN RACE

IDENTIFICATION POINTS

- Smallest tit
- Black head with white cheeks
- Dull colours
- White stripe on nape

CONFUSION SPECIES AND IDENTIFICATION NOTES

Novice birdwatchers can easily confuse the five tits that visit feeders. It only takes a little time to work them out. Here's a quick list to work through:
Great Tit – large with black stripe down yellow belly; Blue Tit – smaller with yellow belly but bright blue crown; Marsh Tit – small, brown with glossy black cap, bib and white cheeks; Willow Tit – like Marsh but non-glossy cap; Coal Tit is smaller still with more black on head and has a white stripe on nape.

CHARACTERISTICS

LENGTH: 10–11.5 cm

WINGSPAN: 17–21 cm

VOICE: A thin, clear 'tsiu or 'tsee', made singularly or repeated. Song 'pitchoo-pitchoo-pitchoo', higher-pitched and faster than Great Tit, often sung from top of tree.

NESTBOX: Yes, especially a tit-box placed in conifers.

NESTING: Always a hole in a variety of places – tree, tree-stump, wall or even in the ground in old rodent burrow. Female builds cup-nest of mosses, grasses and roots. 7–12 red-speckled white eggs laid between April–June. Both parents feed young.

FOOD & FEEDING: Mainly insects and spiders, including caterpillars and grubs. Eats seeds in autumn. Hoards insect and seed food. Uses its slightly long bill to pick out food from under bark and from pine cones. Visits bird-tables, taking food to hide for later use, especially peanuts.

It may be the smallest member of the tit family, but resourceful behaviour and adaptability make the Coal Tit a real survivor. Its small size and relatively longer bill means it can exploit food sources other tits can't reach: it can land on the thinnest of branches and will use its bill to probe and prise open cones or bark. Often bullied at the bird-table and shy by nature, it makes quick smash-and-grab dashes. It also feeds from the ground, from leaves, pine cones or behind bark. If it doesn't find a suitable nest-site in a tree, it will use a hole in the ground instead.

The Coal Tit can be a nervous visitor to the bird-table and is often driven away by Great and Blue Tits. It therefore tends to dash in, grab a peanut and dash off again. Such food is often stashed and revisited when other food supplies are exhausted.

Willow Tit *Poecile montanus*

Occurrence: All year round
Habitats: Mixed woodland, alder and birch scrub, gardens. Absent from Ireland and most of Scotland
Garden ranking: RARE

ADULT Sexes alike

Dull-black cap

Thick neck

Pale panel on wing

Bright-white cheeks

Usually larger bib than Marsh Tit

Whiter cheeks

Grey upperparts

ADULT *BOREALIS* FORM
from northern and eastern Europe

Pale-grey underparts

Pale buff on flanks

IDENTIFICATION POINTS

- Blue Tit-size
- Plain brown with black cap
- Pale cheeks and underparts
- Unlikely to visit bird-tables

CONFUSION SPECIES AND IDENTIFICATION NOTES

Easily confused with Marsh Tit, even by experienced birdwatchers. Luckily their calls are very different. Best features to separate the two, apart from call, are Willow Tit's dull-black cap, pale patch on wing and bright-white cheeks. Blackcaps are much bigger, greyer birds and without the white cheeks.

116

CHARACTERISTICS
LENGTH: 11.5–13 cm
WINGSPAN: 17–20.5 cm
VOICE: Call is a high-pitched 'zee-zee-zee'. Also a harsh, drawn-out 'tchay-tchay-tchay'. The rarely heard song is a melodious 'siu-siu-siu-siu-siu'.
NESTBOX: Yes, especially if filled with wood chip which they can excavate.
NESTING: Female makes nest, chipping at soft rotten wood and then carrying chippings away from site; lines nest with wood chips and soft materials. 6–10 red-speckled white eggs laid between April–June. Both parents feed young.
FOOD & FEEDING: Insects are the main food, but the bill is not as strong as Marsh Tit, so the Willow takes fruit and softer seeds such as alder and birch. Also hoards vast amounts of food for winter months, including insects and spiders. A rare visitor to feeders, but particularly fond of sunflower seeds.

The Willow Tit's claim to fame is that it is one of the most recent British breeding birds to be identified. Due to an error at the Natural History Museum back in 1897, two skins had been incorrectly labelled as the well-known Marsh Tit. Once the proper identification was recognized, separating the two species, it was realised that the Willow Tit was in fact a common British breeding bird. Sadly, this is not the case today; the reasons behind a recent drastic decline in numbers are still unclear.

Unlike the Marsh Tit, the Willow Tit excavates a new nest every year. The soft trunks of rotted alder, willow and birch are favoured nest-sites.

Marsh and Willow Tits are among Britain's least migratory species. They will both join passing tit flocks to forage for food, but soon leave as their territory boundary approaches.

Although they very rarely feed from the ground, Willow Tits often hunt low down in vegetation.

Marsh Tit *Poecile palustris*

Occurrence: All year round
Habitats: Deciduous and mixed (often damp) woods, parks and gardens
Absent from Ireland and most of Scotland
Garden ranking: RARE

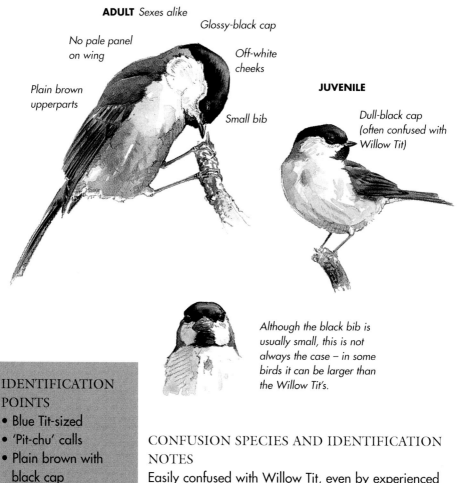

ADULT *Sexes alike*

Glossy-black cap

No pale panel on wing

Off-white cheeks

Plain brown upperparts

JUVENILE

Small bib

Dull-black cap (often confused with Willow Tit)

Although the black bib is usually small, this is not always the case – in some birds it can be larger than the Willow Tit's.

IDENTIFICATION POINTS
- Blue Tit-sized
- 'Pit-chu' calls
- Plain brown with black cap
- Pale cheeks and underparts
- Visits bird-tables

CONFUSION SPECIES AND IDENTIFICATION NOTES

Easily confused with Willow Tit, even by experienced birdwatchers. Luckily, their calls are very different. Look out for Marsh Tit's glossy black cap, lack of pale patch on wing and dirtier white cheeks. Blackcaps are much bigger, greyer birds without white cheeks.

CHARACTERISTICS
LENGTH: 11.5–13 cm
WINGSPAN: 18–19.5 cm
VOICE: Call is an explosive 'pit-chu'. Also a scolding 'pit-chu, chika-dee-dee-dee'. Song is variable, but commonly a repeated single note 'chip-chip-chip'.
NESTBOX: Yes, but rarely.
NESTING: Unlike Willow Tit, it will use existing hole or crevice in tree or wall. Usually low down and lined with moss, hair and grasses. 6–10 red-speckled white eggs laid between April–May. Both parents feed young.
FOOD & FEEDING: Insects are chief food, but also takes seeds from berries in autumn. Will hoard food for winter. Often seen taking whole peanuts in autumn to hide in crack in bark to eat in colder weather when food is scarce. Bird-table behaviour consists of fleeting visits to the table to snatch small seeds and peanuts.

It's impossible to talk about this bird without mentioning its close relative – indeed, almost twin – the Willow Tit. These birds resemble each other so closely it was only in the latter half of the 19th century that they were discovered to be two different species. This is strange, considering that their calls are so distinctively different.

More confusing than their plumage are their names; the Marsh Tit rarely visits marshes and prefers the leafy surrounds of deciduous woodland, whereas the Willow Tit has no strong ties to willow and prefers a mixture of woodland, including coniferous. Marsh Tit numbers have declined rapidly in recent years. It is unclear exactly what the problem is, but it could be due to poor woodland management.

The Marsh Tit's strong bill seems to be used more robustly than the Willow Tit's. Seeds and nuts are held with one foot, whilst hammering with the bill.

Nuthatch *Sitta europaea*

Occurrence: All year round
Habitats: Deciduous mature woodland, especially oak, parks and large gardens. Absent from northern Scotland and Ireland.
Garden ranking: UNCOMMON

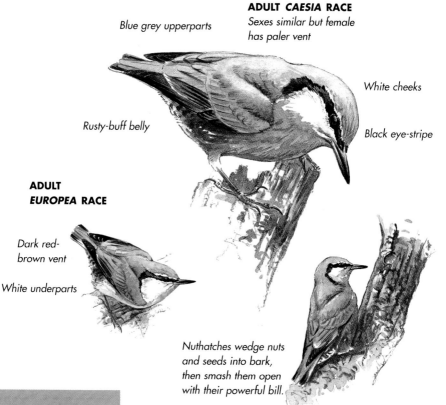

Blue grey upperparts

ADULT *CAESIA* RACE
Sexes similar but female has paler vent

White cheeks

Rusty-buff belly

Black eye-stripe

ADULT EUROPEA RACE

Dark red-brown vent

White underparts

Nuthatches wedge nuts and seeds into bark, then smash them open with their powerful bill.

IDENTIFICATION POINTS
- Looks like small woodpecker
- Creeps up and down trees
- Broad black eye-stripe
- Rusty-buff underparts

CONFUSION SPECIES AND IDENTIFICATION NOTES

At a distance, a small bird creeping along a tree trunk is most likely to be either a Treecreeper or a Nuthatch. If the bird is coming down head-first, then it's a Nuthatch – look out for the broad black eye-stripe. In flight it can look similar to Lesser Spotted Woodpecker.

CHARACTERISTICS

LENGTH: 12–14 cm

WINGSPAN: 22.5–27 cm

VOICE: Various calls, including a clear, loud repeated 'chewitt' or 'twett' becoming louder and more aggressive if alarmed. A rattling 'pee-pee-pee'. Song a falcon-like 'peeu-peeu-peeu' or faster 'wiwiwiwiwiwi'.

NESTBOX: Yes. Enclosed nestbox.

NESTING: Holes in trees or walls; makes entrance smaller by plastering with mud. Lines nest with dried leaves and bark. 6–9 red-speckled white eggs laid between late April–June. Both parents feed young.

FOOD & FEEDING: Insects and spiders are the main summer food, including beetles and grubs. More seeds and nuts are eaten in autumn, with acorns, hazelnuts and beechnuts wedged into bark to be eaten later. Bird-table food includes peanuts (which are also stored), seeds, fat balls and seed log.

There are six types of nuthatch in Europe, but none are as widespread and as approachable as this species, the Eurasian Nuthatch. They are striking birds, and their blustery bravado brightens up any bird-table. The name derives from the old English name 'nut-hack', from their habit of stuffing nuts into tree bark, then hacking at them with their awesome bill until they crack open. The loud smashing sometimes sounds like a woodpecker.

Nuthatches can be hard to find in summer with trees in full leaf, but calls and nut-shells in bark are tell-tale signs. This is one woodland species whose numbers are increasing; their range has expanded, recent warmer winters have meant earlier nesting, and brood sizes have increased.

No other British bird can descend a tree head first. This unique feature separates the Nuthatch from the Treecreeper.

Treecreeper *Certhia familiaris*

Occurrence: All year round

Habitats: Woods, deciduous or mixed, parks and gardens with mature trees.

Garden ranking: RARE

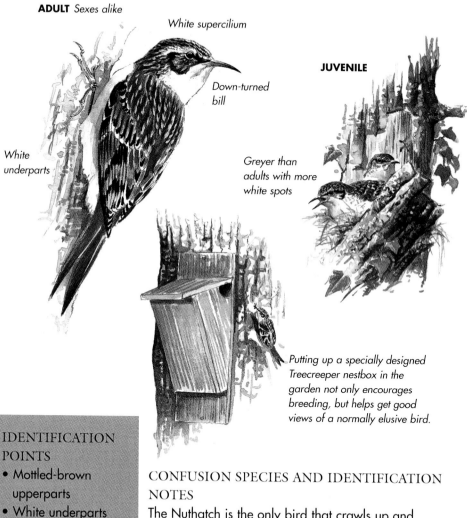

ADULT *Sexes alike*

White supercilium

Down-turned bill

JUVENILE

White underparts

Greyer than adults with more white spots

Putting up a specially designed Treecreeper nestbox in the garden not only encourages breeding, but helps get good views of a normally elusive bird.

IDENTIFICATION POINTS

- Mottled-brown upperparts
- White underparts
- Hops around bark on tree
- Long, down-turned bill

CONFUSION SPECIES AND IDENTIFICATION NOTES

The Nuthatch is the only bird that crawls up and down trees; the Treecreeper can only crawl up, but can't come down head-first. The Short-toed Treecreeper is very similar and occurs in much of southern and western Europe.

122

CHARACTERISTICS

LENGTH: 12.5–14 cm

WINGSPAN: 17.5–21 cm

VOICE: Call is a loud, thin piercing 'zrreeht or zeeit' or 'tsu'. Song has similar tone to Wren – 'tsip-tsee-tsee' – with a thin trill at the end.

NESTBOX: Yes, specially designed wedge-shaped box.

NESTING: In holes or cracks in trees, ivy-covered walls, usually behind bark in dead tree. Male finds the site and female builds nest, lining hole with dead twigs and other soft materials. 6–9 eggs with brown flecks, usually at large end, laid between April–June. Both parents feed young.

FOOD & FEEDING: Almost exclusively insects and spiders plucked from bark, including earwigs, caterpillars and flies. Eats seeds in winter. Rarely visits bird-tables, but can be encouraged if bark is smeared with fat and seeds.

The Treecreeper is perfectly adapted to a life spent exclusively in trees. It rarely lands on the ground as it gets everything it needs from its arboreal home. Its sharp claws are suitable for clinging onto bark, and its long down-turned bill enables it to scrape away at bark and winkle out insects from the cracks. The strong, rusty-brown tail is used for balance as it hops along the bark. To avoid detection by larger predators, its mottled upperparts act as very effective camouflage, sometimes too much so when you are looking for them!

There is a method to their mouse-like creeping on trees; they fly to the bottom of the trunk, hop with both feet in a spiral path up and around the trunk. As soon as they've had enough, they fly off to the bottom of the next tree.

As for many small birds, harsh winters can be fatal for Treecreepers. They not only build winter nests behind bark but also often use specially designed nestboxes. During the winter they frequently join roving tit flocks.

123

Jay *Garrulus glandarius*

Occurrence: All year round

Habitats: Woods of any kind, hedgerows, wooded parks and anywhere with acorns. Absent from northern Scotland and south-west Ireland.

Garden ranking: UNCOMMON

ADULT *Sexes alike*

Streaked crown

Pinkish-brown upperparts

Black moustache

White throat

Black tail

Light blue patch in wing

White rump

Broad, rounded wings

Fluttering, slow flight

During courtship or when annoyed, they raise their crest

IDENTIFICATION POINTS
- Large pink-brown bird
- White rump in sweeping flight
- Jackdaw-sized
- Blue in wing

CONFUSION SPECIES AND IDENTIFICATION NOTES

Although the Jay is a highly distinctive bird, a Hoopoe in flight can look similar.

CHARACTERISTICS
LENGTH: 34–35 cm
WINGSPAN: 52–58 cm
VOICE: Calls are hoarse, raucous screams 'scaaarg-scaaarg'. Also a descending mew 'piyeh', similar to Buzzard. Song is a mixture of chuckles, knocking and mewing.
NESTBOX: No.
NESTING: Both adults build nest of twigs, roots, hair and mud usually on branch or fork of tree in well-hidden location. 3–7 green eggs with brown flecks laid between May–June. Both parents feed young.
FOOD & FEEDING: Almost anything, from insects, reptiles, amphibians, small birds and nestlings to fruit and nuts but favourite food is certainly acorns, which it hides to eat throughout the year. Visits bird-tables.

As big as a Jackdaw with pinkish-brown feathers and electric blue flashes, yet difficult to see well. The Jay is usually a very shy bird, only visiting bird-tables when it's quiet; very early morning is the best time to see them. In September and November, they rush around parks and gardens in a flurry of acorn-collecting activity, part of their forward-planning for the winter. One bird can collect up to five thousand acorns during this period! If the Jay doesn't have oak trees in its territory, it will make repeated journeys to trees elsewhere, returning to stash the food – lawns and woodland borders are the usual places. Jays are the greatest dispersers of acorns, thereby promoting a new generation of oak trees.

When you hear harsh 'scaaaarg, scaaarg' screams coming from the woods, it could one or more excitable Jays trying to persuade a roosting owl or some other threat to move on.

125

Magpie *Pica pica*

Occurrence: All year round
Habitats: Woods, farmland, hedges, coastal bushes, gardens and moorland
Absent from northern Scotland.
Garden ranking: COMMON

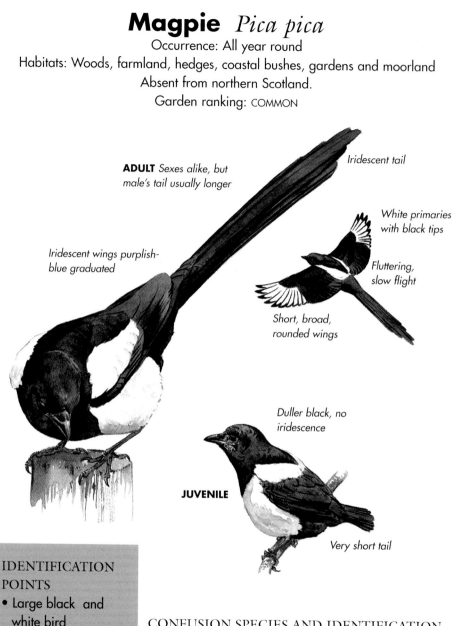

ADULT *Sexes alike, but male's tail usually longer*

Iridescent tail

White primaries with black tips

Iridescent wings purplish-blue graduated

Fluttering, slow flight

Short, broad, rounded wings

Duller black, no iridescence

JUVENILE

Very short tail

IDENTIFICATION POINTS
• Large black and white bird
• Long graduated tail
• Jerky walk
• Fluttering flight

CONFUSION SPECIES AND IDENTIFICATION NOTES
The Magpie is unmistakable. The only other Magpie that occurs in Europe is the Azure-winged Magpie in Spain and Portugal, but it looks very different.

CHARACTERISTICS

LENGTH: 44–46 cm, of which 20–30 cm is tail

WINGSPAN: 52–60 cm

VOICE: Most common call is a fast, loud and laughing 'chak-chak-chak-chak'; also makes other chattering and piping notes, especially when breeding.

NESTBOX: No.

NESTING: Large, dome-shaped nest of branches and twigs, with side entrance; made by both parents. Nest-building can start in mid-winter. 5–7 greenish or brownish eggs with darker flecks, laid between March–May. Both parents feed young for up to six weeks after fledging.

FOOD & FEEDING: Almost anything, from insects, small mammals, reptiles and amphibians to other birds' nestlings, carrion, fruit and seeds. Can quickly clean up bird-tables.

Magpies are great architects, making large, strong nests; some have roofs to keep out the weather and aerial predators.

The Magpie has an undeserved bad reputation, and it's a great shame that a bird of such character, beauty and intelligence is treated as a villain and a pest. Game-keepers still trap and kill Magpies as the birds are thought to deplete pheasant and partridge chick numbers. While the Magpie is certainly guilty of taking eggs and nestlings, these only make up a small part of its varied diet.

Magpie numbers have increased in recent years as persecution has decreased and the birds have adapted to life in urban areas. Non-breeding birds sometimes gather in flocks of up to twenty; such groups are called 'Magpie parliaments'.

127

Jackdaw *Corvus monedula*

Occurrence: All year round
Habitats: Woodland, cliffs, urban areas and farmland
Garden ranking: LESS COMMON

ADULT *Sexes alike*

*Silver-grey nape
dark forehead*

Pale eye

Dark legs

Short bill

The fun-loving
nature of Jackdaws
is obvious when
you see them
playing around
in the air and
showing incredible
acrobatic prowess.

Warm chimney-pots can help
against the winter chill. During
the day the birds are out feeding
on fields, tips etc, but by night they
return to the safety of the roof.

IDENTIFICATION POINTS

- Smallest crow
- Silvery-grey neck
- Upright, clockwork walk
- Pale-grey eye

CONFUSION SPECIES AND IDENTIFICATION NOTES

All black birds of the crow family, *Corvidae*, are
'crows' to non-birdwatchers. Compared to Jackdaws,
Carrion Crows are larger and all black; Rooks are all
black, but with a pale-grey bill.

128

LENGTH: 33–34 cm
WINGSPAN: 67–74 cm
VOICE: Call is a characteristic 'chak'; also an excitable 'chaka-chaka-chak".
NESTBOX: Yes. Large enclosed nestbox; also chimneys.
NESTING: Always in loose colonies, nests in holes in buildings, cliffs, trees, even rabbit burrows. Both parents build nest of twigs, lined with mixture of materials, fur, hair, wool. 4 or 5 pale blue eggs laid between April–June. Both parents feed young.
FOOD & FEEDING: Varied diet, but eats more seed and plant materials than other corvids. Forages on the ground for insects; also eats fruit, berries, young birds and eggs. Will take almost anything off the bird-table!

Intelligent, resourceful, neat, acrobatic, sociable and full of character – just a few words that describe this amazing bird. If you haven't seen or watched a Jackdaw before, put down this book and go and find one. It's not often you see one on its own; the monogamous pairs travel everywhere together. They not only join up with other Jackdaws, but also with flocks of Rooks and Carrion Crows.

Jackdaws have a jerky, upright walk but can also hop. Their love of shiny, precious things has landed them in all sorts of trouble, with nests found full of bits of tin foil and other glittering items, including stashes of earrings and other jewellery. It doesn't take long for a Jackdaw to become semi-tame; with regular feeding these plucky, fearless birds will become your best mates!

Holes are the preferred nest-site, either in trees or buildings. Chimneys make an excellent substitute to tree holes, but this can be a nuisance if you plan to use your fireplace!

Rook *Corvus frugilegus*

Occurrence: All year round
Habitats: Open woodland, agricultural land and parkland
Garden ranking: RARE

JUVENILE

Dark brown

Dark bill

Feathered face

Peak-shaped crown

Steep forehead

ADULT
Sexes alike

Slender pointed bill

Pale base to bill

Hang a bone from a visible spot and watch a Rook or any other corvid show off its surprising agility as it tries to get at the marrow.

IDENTIFICATION FEATURES

- Large, black bird
- Pale-grey base to bill
- Nests in rookeries

CONFUSION SPECIES AND IDENTIFICATION NOTES

Confused with Carrion Crows due to similar size, but Rook has bigger, pale bill and is usually seen in large flocks. Jackdaws are much smaller and have grey napes.

130

CHARACTERISTICS

LENGTH: 44–46 cm

WINGSPAN: 81–99 cm

VOICE: Call is a nasal, raucous 'kaah'. Song is a mixture of soft caws, croaks and squeaks.

NESTBOX: No.

NESTING: In colonies from two nests to over a thousand. Males select site, both birds build large nest of twigs, grasses and mud in tops of trees. 3–5 greenish eggs with brown mottling, laid between late February–June. Both parents feed young, male brings brooding female food stored in its pouch.

FOOD & FEEDING: Earthworms are its chief food, but grain and insects are also taken, including leatherjackets (crane-fly larvae), beetles and caterpillars, as well as fruit, carrion, eggs and nestlings. Food is carried in an extendable throat pouch. Will visit a bird-table in search of meaty scraps.

Rooks are the most sociable members of the crow family. For anyone living within earshot of a rookery, the noise of their rowdy, communal nesting habits can be deafening, but the compensation comes from watching their fantastic display flights and their intriguing social interactions. Rookeries can be used either throughout the year or just at breeding time.

Rooks are unlikely to stray far into cities and other built-up areas, as they prefer open fields to search for invertebrates. Although wary of humans (due to persecution) they will visit bird-feeders, taking pretty much anything on offer. The large amount of pest insects they eat should be considered before mass persecutions, such as Rook shoots, are carried out.

The communal nest-sites, called rookeries, are a familiar sight in open farmland. Display flights and noisy squabbles are commonplace.

131

Carrion Crow and Hooded Crow
Corvus corone & C.cornix

Occurrence: All year round
Habitats: Woodland edge, farmland, moorland, coastal and urban areas,
replaced by Hooded Crow, *C. cornix*, in northern Britain and Europe
Garden ranking: LESS COMMON

ADULT
Sexes alike

Rounded crown

ADULT HOODED CROW, C. CORNIX

Black head, breast and wings

Stocky, dark bill

Grey upper- and underparts

Birds of prey and Grey Herons are seen as a threat. Repeated mobbing and even body strikes by flocks or even a single crow soon persuade the intruder to leave.

IDENTIFICATION FEATURES
- All black with dark bill (Carrion)
- Contrasting grey and black plumage (Hooded)
- Often seen singly or pairs
- In flight shows broad wings with 'fingers'

CONFUSION SPECIES AND IDENTIFICATION NOTES
Rooks have paler bills and appear less stocky than crows. The Hooded Crow is a separate species, and replaces the Carrion Crow in northern Britain and most of Europe. The two interbreed where ranges overlap, creating black crows with suggestions of grey in various parts but not so contrasting as in pure Hoodeds. Jackdaws are smaller, with a grey nape.

CHARACTERISTICS

LENGTH: 45–47 cm

WINGSPAN: 93–104 cm

VOICE: A variety of harsh, raucous calls, including familiar, rolling 'kraa-kraa-kraa'. When mobbing, gives grating 'krrra' and 'ark-ark' calls repeated in quick succession.

NESTBOX: No.

NESTING: Both parents build a substantial nest of twigs and small branches high in trees, cliffs or pylons; lined with softer materials. Male brings food and stands guard for brooding female. 4–5 greenish eggs with brown mottling are laid between March–June. Both parents feed young, who stay with parents for up to 6 months after fledging.

FOOD & FEEDING: Almost anything, including insects, grain, fruit, vegetables, grubs, carrion, shellfish, bones, young birds, injured or struggling animals, eggs and human waste. Will visit bird-tables, taking meaty scraps, bread and pretty much anything you put out.

Research shows that crows are among the most intelligent of birds and watching them for any length of time soon reveals how skilful they are. Aesop observed their resourceful nature in his fable *The Crow and the Pitcher*, where the thirsty crow threw in pebbles to raise the water level. Crows quickly exploit new foods, and are great fun to watch as they struggle with a dangling bone in the garden.

There isn't much food that the resourceful Crow can't eat. Even food with a hard casing, such as bones and crabs, are dropped from a height so they smash open and the meat is revealed.

Unfairly regarded as a bird of bad omen by humans, crows are understandably wary, so close views can be difficult to get. They are regarded as a pest and are regularly shot on farmland. The major cause for concern is their predation of the nests of rare breeding birds such as Capercaillie and Black Grouse.

Starling *Sturnus vulgaris*

Occurrence: All year round
Habitats: Towns, cities, farmland and cliffs
Garden ranking: COMMON

ADULT SUMMER PLUMAGE
Sexes alike, but male has
blue-grey base to bill

Sharp yellow bill

By late summer,
juveniles start to grow
into their adult
feathers; this
mixed messy
plumage
lasts over
winter.

Dark bill

Pale chin

Purple and green
iridescence

Short tail

JUVENILE

Heavily spotted all over

**ADULT WINTER
PLUMAGE**

IDENTIFICATION FEATURES

- Dark, shiny bird with yellow bill
- Smaller, thinner than Blackbird
- Often in noisy groups
- Arrow-shape in flight

CONFUSION SPECIES AND IDENTIFICATION NOTES

At a distance you might mistake one for a Blackbird. Starlings are more upright, have a jerky walk and shorter tail. Similar shape to a Waxwing in flight. Two other starlings occur in Europe; Rose-coloured Starling is a rare visitor to UK, usually juveniles and winter birds. Spotless Starlings replace the Starling in Spain and northern Africa.

CHARACTERISTICS

LENGTH: 19–21.5 cm

WINGSPAN: 37–42 cm

VOICE: Repertoire of trills, whistles, chirps and 'churring'. Gifted in mimicry, often imitating any nearby birdsong; can even emulate telephones and occasionally wolf-whistles.

NESTBOX: Yes. Large enclosed box.

NESTING: Male builds rough nest then sings while shivering his wings to attract female; she finishes the nest. Male may have more than one mate, and females may lay eggs in others' nests. Nests in holes in trees or buildings. 4 or 5 pale blue-green eggs laid between April–May. Both parents feed young.

FOOD & FEEDING: Leatherjackets (crane-fly larvae) and earthworms are the chief food, although a variety of other foods is eaten. Probes open grassland, lawns and playing fields with its long bill. Other insects, fruit and seeds also taken. Regular visitor to the bird-table, taking a variety of scraps.

Although still a common garden bird, the Starling has undergone a worrying decrease in numbers in recent years. As yet there is no clear explanation for this, although the reduction in open pasture and changing farming practices could both be factors. The Starling is possibly one of our most entertaining garden birds; they live in flocks and are constantly chatting, squabbling and interacting with each other.

As their bills are not designed for carrying large amounts of food to the nest, parent Starlings bring their young to the ground as soon as possible. They then put the food directly into the youngster's mouths.

Communal roosts can be large, sometimes numbering thousands of birds. In winter our own resident Starlings are joined by millions from northern Europe, where they are summer visitors. Many roosts are in cities where, after a cold day feeding out in the fields, Starlings can find warmth and a safe refuge.

House Sparrow *Passer domesticus*

Occurrence: All year round
Habitats: Built-up areas, farmyards and scrub
Garden ranking: VERY COMMON

MALE

Grey crown, cheeks

Darker bill

Black throat and breast

Summer males have more black on breast

FEMALE

Cream supercilium

Pale bill (darker in summer)

Juveniles are very similar to females, but their colours are a bit brighter, with a darker crown and a yellowish bill.

Dirty brown-grey underparts

IDENTIFICATION FEATURES

- Grey crown & cheeks on males
- Females duller all over
- Often in low bushes, buildings
- Noisy chirps and twitters

CONFUSION SPECIES AND IDENTIFICATION NOTES

Females can be confused with female Chaffinches; look out for the white markings on a Chaffinch's wing. Tree Sparrows differ from male House Sparrows as they have a brown crown and white cheeks with a black spot.

CHARACTERISTICS
LENGTH: 14–15 cm
WINGSPAN: 21–25.5 cm
VOICE: Call is a mixture of chirping and chattering. Song similar to calls, 'chip, chip, chippi, chip'. When agitated, a rattling 'cherrrrr'.
NESTBOX: Yes. Enclosed nestboxes.
NESTING: Prefers holes in trees or buildings, with eaves and thatched roofs frequently used. Likes to nest in colonies, and couples continue to roost in nest throughout year. Untidy nest of straw, grass and feathers. 2–4 brown-blotched white eggs laid between March–September. Both parents feed young.
FOOD & FEEDING: Essentially a seed-eater, but also eats insects, flowers, grasses and seeds. Can visit bird-tables en masse, creating havoc.

Although in 2005 the House Sparrow emerged as the commonest garden bird in the RSPB's *Garden Bird Survey*, over the last 30 years Britain's sparrow population has fallen from around twelve million to just six million. In London, where the species was once ubiquitous, seven out of ten sparrows have disappeared.

If you want to encourage sparrows to dust-bathe in your garden, build a shallow pit and fill it with sand and dusty soil. Dust-bathing helps rid the birds of parasites and keeps feathers clean.

The exact reason for this fall is still unknown. However, lack of insects during the breeding season (to feed the young nestlings) may be one reason, as is a lack of suitable nest-sites. Meanwhile, in some areas of Britain and Europe the House Sparrow is doing very well; more research is needed to establish just what is going on with the most familiar and appealing of our garden birds.

137

Tree Sparrow *Passer montanus*

Occurrence: All year round

Habitats: Arable farmland, open woodland, gardens and parks. Absent from the far north of Scotland.

Garden ranking: RARE

ADULT *Sexes alike*

Rounded head

Red-brown cap

Black bib

Two wing-bars

Grey-brown cap

JUVENILE

Pale collar, white cheeks with black mark

Grey cheeks

During courtship birds run along branches with tail up and bill thrust forward; the recipient politely bows to show acceptance.

IDENTIFICATION FEATURES
- Like House Sparrow but with brown cap
- White cheeks and collar
- Black spot on white cheek
- Two white wingbars

CONFUSION SPECIES AND IDENTIFICATION NOTES

Male House Sparrows don't have the chestnut-brown cap or white cheeks, and they have grey underparts while Tree Sparrows are buff-brown. In Europe, Spanish Sparrows, *P. hispaniolensis*, can look similar but are darker with streaks on both upper- and underparts.

HARACTERISTICS
LENGTH: 12.5–14 cm
WINGSPAN: 20–22 cm
VOICE: Call is 'chip', higher-pitched than House Sparrow. In flight, a dry, fast 'tek, tek'. Song is a fast variable collection of 'tsvits'.
NESTBOX: Yes. Enclosed nestboxes.
NESTING: Always in holes in trees, cliffs, buildings. Takes over tit-boxes, even with the tit chicks still present, by simply piling nesting material on top. Dry grasses and leaves are placed in the hole. Both parents build nest. 2–7 mottled-brown eggs laid between late April–August.
FOOD & FEEDING: Eats both a wide variety of seeds, from weeds and grasses, and also insects, which it collects from the ground, leaves and even on the wing.

The Tree Sparrow was once a common countryside bird, but in Britain they have declined dramatically. Elsewhere in Europe, Tree Sparrow numbers are stable, so it would seem the drastic reduction in Britain is due to the changing nature of the British countryside.

This hole-nesting species readily uses artificial nestboxes.

Intensive farming and autumn sowing affects any bird on a diet of grasses, cereals or weed seeds (and insects for their young) and so may explain the Tree Sparrow's decline. Unlike House Sparrows, they usually prefer quiet rural areas and the best places to find them nowadays are near lowland farmyards, where spilt grain and animal food make quick and easy meals.

Although not a native New World species, in 1870 about 24 birds were released in LaFayette Park, St Louis, Missouri; now there are around 150,000 in this part of the USA.

Chaffinch *Fringilla coelebs*

Occurrence: All year round
Habitats: Any type of woodland, parks, gardens and farmland
Garden ranking: VERY COMMON

MALE, SUMMER PLUMAGE

Blue-grey head

Flight is undulating, with two distinctive white wing-bars.

Pink cheeks and breast

White in wing

FEMALE

No clear supercilium (as with female House Sparrow)

The white in the wings is a good way to tell it apart from the female House Sparrow.

Forked tail

Paler cheeks

White in tail

IDENTIFICATION POINTS

- Male has pink breast, grey cap
- Females brown with white in wing and tail
- Two white wingbars in flight

CONFUSION SPECIES AND IDENTIFICATION NOTES

The Brambling's habits and markings can confuse. However, the male Brambling has a dark head and orange underparts, and the female has more colour than the female Chaffinch. Females do resemble female House Sparrows, but have white in the wing.

CHARACTERISTICS

LENGTH: 14.5–16 cm

WINGSPAN: 24.5–28.5 cm

VOICE: Calls vary – a perky 'frink', a nasal 'te-eup' and 'huitt', repeated persistently, and a softer 'yup' in flight. Song is fast and trilling with a flourish at the end.

NESTBOX: No.

NESTING: Lichen-covered cup-nest of grass and moss, lined with feathers and small roots; built by female. 3–5 pale brown or green eggs with pink-brown smudges laid between May–August. Nests in fork of bush or tree.

FOOD & FEEDING: A wide variety of seeds and beechmast, also eats insects in summer, especially caterpillars when feeding young. Making fewer visits to the bird-table than you'd imagine, Chaffinches prefer to hop around below picking up scraps.

The Chaffinch is one of the UK's most numerous species. Many British birds are sedentary, rarely moving more than a few miles from where they were hatched. However, from October they are joined by northern European Chaffinches escaping the severe Scandinavian winter.

Their habit of feeding on the ground, especially under feeders, means they are in constant danger of a cat attack. Research has shown cat-collars emitting special sound waves can drastically reduce fatalities.

Although the male's plumage is more subdued in winter, he still looks impressive. Chaffinches flock together in winter and if beechmast is available, large groups can be seen feeding on the ground – they look a little like clockwork toys, jerking their heads about as they hop along. Mixed winter flocks of Chaffinches, Bramblings and Tree Sparrows frequently feed together in arable fields.

Brambling *Fringilla montifringilla*

Occurrence: Winter visitor between September–March
Habitats: Woodland, especially beech, but also farmland and yards
Garden ranking: RARE

MALE, WINTER PLUMAGE

Grey-brown head and grey nape

Forked tail

White belly

Orange shoulders

Yellow bill

MALE, SUMMER PLUMAGE

Black bill

Glossy black head

White rump

Almost all-black tail

FEMALE

Brown cheeks

Dark brown scalloping

Grey underparts

IDENTIFICATION POINTS
- Black head (males)
- Orange shoulders and breast
- White rump and belly
- Large flocks in winter

CONFUSION SPECIES AND IDENTIFICATION NOTES
Chaffinches and Bramblings share many features but plumage-wise, Bramblings have generally warmer, orangey-brown tones, less white in the wing and a noticeable white rump.

142

CHARACTERISTICS
LENGTH: 14 cm
WINGSPAN: 25–26 cm
VOICE: Call is a loud squeaky, nasal 'tee-up'. 'Yeck' calls in flight. Slow, wheezing song is rarely heard in the UK.
NESTBOX: No.
NESTING: Larger and messier than Chaffinch, usually found in the fork of a tree (usually birch, also spruce). Very rare breeder in northern Britain, but common in birch forest in Fenno-Scandia. 6–7 eggs laid, both parents rear young.
FOOD & FEEDING: Predominantly a ground-feeding seed-eater, with beechmast the most popular winter food. Also takes weeds, pine seeds, berries and grain. Summer food includes insects, which it can catch on the wing. Regularly visits gardens and feeders in favoured spots.

Next time you dismiss a flock of feeding finches rising up from fallen beechmast as simply Chaffinches, just check again. Among them you could have missed a Brambling. A close look as they fly off may reveal the characteristic white rump of the bird known as the 'Northern Chaffinch'. Feeding flocks are easily spooked; they tend to fly off together then return pretty quickly to the same spot, once the danger has passed.

Bramblings annually invade western Europe to escape the harsh northern European winter. Sometimes their numbers reach the millions, but this is unusual. Most of the birds we see in the UK are in their winter plumage, but occasionally birds arriving in late summer are still in their bright breeding plumage. The best place to find them is around a beech tree, on open farmland or in woods. Gardens with trees and feeders can attract Bramblings – keep checking those Chaffinches!

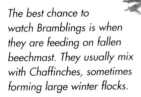

The best chance to watch Bramblings is when they are feeding on fallen beechmast. They usually mix with Chaffinches, sometimes forming large winter flocks.

Greenfinch *Carduelis chloris*

Occurrence: All year round
Habitats: Hedgerows, gardens and woodland edge
Garden ranking: VERY COMMON

MALE

Yellow panel in wing

Notched tail with yellow on edges

Thick, pale bill

Yellowy-green breast

JUVENILE

Grey-white streaks

Pale-yellow panel in wing and tail edge

Pale streaks all over

FEMALE

Pale greyish-green chest

Brown, faintly streaked upperparts

Yellow panel in wing

Pale yellow on tail edge

IDENTIFICATION POINTS
• Predominantly green
• Yellow panels in wings
• Yellow tail in flight

CONFUSION SPECIES AND IDENTIFICATION NOTES
Siskins and Serins share similar colours, but the Greenfinch's plumage lacks their contrast and it is a bigger, heavier bird.

CHARACTERISTICS

LENGTH: 14–16 cm

WINGSPAN: 24.5–27.5 cm

VOICE: Calls are a rasping 'sweee' and in flight a hard 'jupp, jupp, jupp'. Song is a mixture of twittering trills and wheezy notes.

NESTBOX: No.

NESTING: Bulky cup-nest of twigs, grasses, moss, lined with hair and fine stems. Birds sometimes nest in colonies of up to 6 birds in a small tree. 4–6 red-spotted cream eggs laid between April–August. Both parents feed young.

FOOD & FEEDING: Grain and seeds, including dandelion, burdock, groundsel, yew and various seeds from feeders. Peanuts and sunflower seeds are a particular favourite; Greenfinches will readily dominate feeders to get at them.

A summer-plumaged male bird in bright sunlight is a beautiful sight, a stunning rich-green colour and with contrasting yellow in the wing. They are also fun to watch, especially at the bird-table. Aggressive if challenged, they won't think twice about seeing off tits. The dynamics between Great Tits and Greenfinches are fascinating, as both birds engage in threat displays and will frequently challenge one another – often with neither bird emerging as a clear winner.

The urban Greenfinch population has increased recently, perhaps due to a reduction in countryside food. The repetitive dry, rasping 'swee' of the male Greenfinch can be a little tiring after a while, but his fluttering song-flight easily makes up for this. He repeatedly circles the treetops on slow, bat-like wing-beats, calling as he flies.

Out of the breeding season Greenfinches move in small groups. Be prepared for noisy visits once they discover your feeders – peanuts and seeds are equally popular.

Goldfinch *Carduelis carduelis*

Occurrence: All year round, partial migrant
Habitats: Weedy fields, neglected areas, gardens and scrub; also coastal.
Garden ranking: LESS COMMON

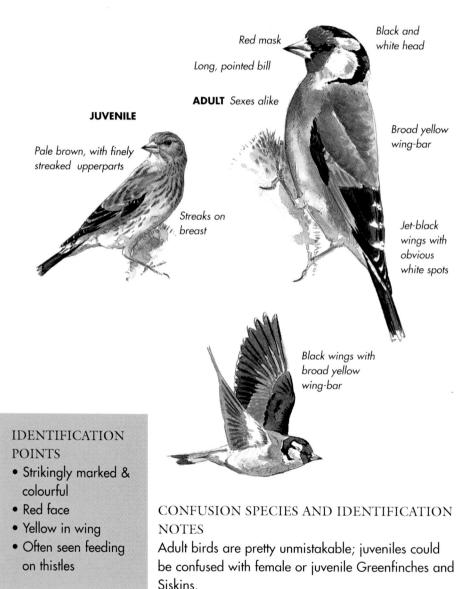

Red mask

Long, pointed bill

Black and white head

ADULT *Sexes alike*

JUVENILE

Pale brown, with finely streaked upperparts

Broad yellow wing-bar

Streaks on breast

Jet-black wings with obvious white spots

Black wings with broad yellow wing-bar

IDENTIFICATION POINTS
• Strikingly marked & colourful
• Red face
• Yellow in wing
• Often seen feeding on thistles

CONFUSION SPECIES AND IDENTIFICATION NOTES
Adult birds are pretty unmistakable; juveniles could be confused with female or juvenile Greenfinches and Siskins.

CHARACTERISTICS
LENGTH: 12 cm
WINGSPAN: 21–25.5 cm
VOICE: Calls are liquid and twittering, and include an excited 'switt-wit-wit' in flight. Song is a mixture of random, liquid twittering notes.
NESTBOX: No.
NESTING: Female builds a delicate, well-hidden cup-nest, lined with thistle down, usually towards the end of a branch and sometimes communally. 4–6 red-speckled eggs are laid between April–August. Parents feed young for about a week after fledging.
FOOD & FEEDING: Chief food is seeds; their relatively long bill is perfect for pulling seeds from weeds, including thistle, dandelion, teasel and groundsel. They also eat insects during the breeding season. Increasingly common on garden feeders, where seeds such as nyjer and sunflower are eagerly taken.

Historically, its beauty and song has been the Goldfinch's biggest problem. As far back as the 1600s Goldfinches were caught and harnessed for their song, either in a cage or by a thin chain to one of their legs. As if this were not enough, the Victorians used to blind the birds before caging them, believing that blind birds sang louder and more often. Thomas Hardy was so incensed by this barbaric practice that he wrote a poem about it.

The collective noun for Goldfinches is a 'charm', a befitting word for such a gorgeous bird. The best way to encourage them into your garden is to fill your feeders with seeds and also leave a weedy area, especially with thistles. Their scientific name *carduelis* means thistle in Latin, and their bill is perfectly designed to extract seeds from such thistle seed-heads.

Goldfinches are among the most colourful birds you can attract to your garden. Nyjer seeds and sunflower hearts are their favourite food.

Siskin *Carduelis spinus*

Occurrence: All year round, but migrants arrive in autumn/winter
Habitats: Gardens, conifer plantations, alder and birch woods.
Garden ranking: UNCOMMON

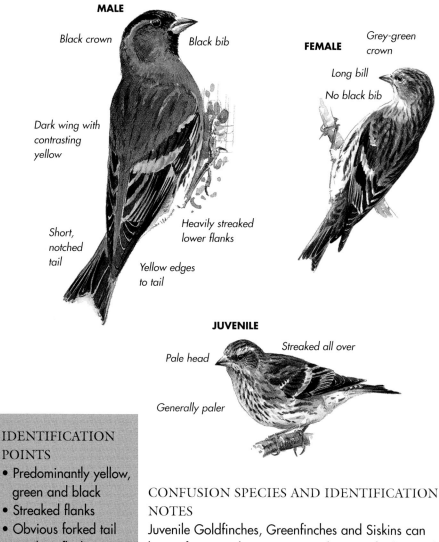

MALE

Black crown

Black bib

FEMALE

Grey-green crown

Long bill

No black bib

Dark wing with contrasting yellow

Short, notched tail

Heavily streaked lower flanks

Yellow edges to tail

JUVENILE

Streaked all over

Pale head

Generally paler

IDENTIFICATION POINTS
• Predominantly yellow, green and black
• Streaked flanks
• Obvious forked tail
• Feeds in flocks

CONFUSION SPECIES AND IDENTIFICATION NOTES
Juvenile Goldfinches, Greenfinches and Siskins can be confusing to the novice. Female Greenfinches and the rare Serin also need to be ruled out.

CHARACTERISTICS

LENGTH: 11–12 cm

WINGSPAN: 20–23 cm

VOICE: Call – often heard in flight – is a shrill 'tsew' or ringing 'tszing'. Song is twittering, with a drawn-out wheezing note at the end.

NESTBOX: No.

NESTING: Nest is small and compact, usually built towards the end of a branch. Nests in conifers and mixed woodland, preferring to have alder and birch nearby for food. 3–5 red-streaked, pale blue eggs laid between May–August.

FOOD & FEEDING: A seed-eater, preferring spruce and pine as well as alder and birch. Also takes seeds from weeds and is an increasingly common visitor to gardens for seeds and peanuts. Eats insects in the breeding season.

Although these lively, acrobatic finches are here all year round, more are seen in winter when many leave woodland to visit garden seed-feeders. In late autumn, even more arrive from northern Europe, preferring the UK's warmer winters and thus boosting numbers. They sometimes arrive in large numbers if their food supply further north fails.

Watching Siskins in the garden is very rewarding. Probably the most agile of all finches, their behaviour could easily be confused with a tit, as they hang upside-down on feeders and flit with elegance through the garden.

Although Siskin numbers fluctuate due to the migrants, the population seems to be experiencing a slight rise; this could be due to the maturing of forestry plantations planted after the Second World War.

Winter Siskin flocks frequently visit garden feeders, where you can marvel at their acrobatic skills and striking plumage.

Linnet *Carduelis cannabina*

Occurrence: All year round
Habitats: Farmland, roadsides, neglected ground, gorse and heath.
Garden ranking: RARE

MALE, SUMMER PLUMAGE

Red crown

Short, grey bill

Grey head

Red breast

Brown back

Longish tail

FEMALE

Lacks red crown and breast

Grey-brown nape

Dark-brown upperparts

Pale underparts

Almost identical to female, but generally duller brown upperparts and more heavily streaked

JUVENILE

IDENTIFICATION POINTS
- Bright red on forehead and breast (males)
- Rarely seen singularly
- Rises in hopping flight from the ground
- Restless large winter flocks

CONFUSION SPECIES AND IDENTIFICATION NOTES

A male in full summer plumage is easy to identify, once you've ruled out the smaller, streaky Lesser Redpoll and the rarer Common Rosefinch! Female Linnets can be difficult, especially next to Twite (not a garden bird) and Redpoll; look for the grey nape and bill.

CHARACTERISTICS
LENGTH: 12.5–13.5 cm
WINGSPAN: 21–25.5 cm
VOICE: Call is a dry, nasal 'tig-itt' or 'teet-eet-eet'. Song is a pleasing mixture of
fast rattling notes and warbles, with some whistling.
NESTBOX: No.
NESTING: Female builds cup-nest low to the ground, lined with hair and wool;
in gorse and bramble especially. 4–6 bluish-white eggs laid between April–June.
FOOD & FEEDING: Chief food is seeds, especially weeds such as dandelion,
chickweeds and fat hen. Oil-seed rape is also popular. A small amount of insects
are taken while breeding.

The urban birdwatcher may be unfamiliar with this bird, as open farmland and heaths are its favourite habitat. However, as weedy fields have become more scarce due to intensive farming, Linnets are moving into suburban areas. Like Goldfinches, they were also once kept as cagebirds for their bright colours and melodious songs, with vast numbers being trapped and sold until the trade was outlawed.

In the 1970s a decline in the Linnet population began, due mainly to agricultural changes. Numbers remain down, but the increased planting of oil-seed rape has provided an important new source of food for Linnets. Together with the introduction of incentives for farmers to farm in a more 'wildlife-friendly' way, this may help save this attractive finch.

Oil-seed rape has thrown a life-line to the endangered Linnet. Adult birds can just about find enough seeds from weeds such as dandelion to feed their first brood; for the second brood, the rape seeds provide a bumper harvest.

151

Lesser Redpoll *Carduelis cabaret*

Occurrence: All year round, migrants arrive in autumn/winter
Habitats: Woodland, parkland and heathland
Garden ranking: RARE

MALE

Red forehead

Warm brown
upperparts

Small, yellow bill

Pale-pink rump

Black lores and chin

Pale wing bars

Small amount of red
on forehead

JUVENILE

Streaked-
brown rump

FEMALE

No red on
forehead

Generally
paler, usually
lacking pink
on underparts

IDENTIFICATION POINTS

- Small, round bird with notched tail
- Red mark on forehead
- Heavily streaked
- Feeds in flocks

CONFUSION SPECIES AND IDENTIFICATION NOTES

Common Redpolls *C. flammea* look very similar; they are slightly larger and more grey-brown than the Lessers. Twites (not a garden species) lack the red forehead. Female Linnets lack the heavy streaks and red forehead.

CHARACTERISTICS
LENGTH: 11.5–14 cm
WINGSPAN: 20–25 cm
VOICE: Call is a buzzing 'jeet-jeet-jeet' and a repetitive trill in flight. Song is a twittering 'chi-chi-chi'.
NESTBOX: No.
NESTING: Untidy cup-nest of twigs and stems, lined with thistle down, hair and feathers. Usually high up in a bush, but occasionally low to the ground. Nests in loose communities, preferring birch and gorse. 4–5 white-blue eggs with dark flecks laid between April–August.
FOOD & FEEDING: A seed-eater; chief seed is birch, then alder. Also eats flowers and seeds from low-growing plants such as willowherbs, sorrel and tansy. Eats insects in breeding season.

For the novice birdwatcher, redpolls are difficult to sort out and even advanced birders struggle with their identification. The two redpolls that regularly occur in the UK are the Common (or Mealy) *C. flammea* and the Lesser, *C. cabaret*. The Lesser breeds here while the Common is a sporadic winter visitor from northern Europe; the two have only recently been split into separate species.

Acting more like tits than finches, they acrobatically flit from branch to branch, busily searching for food. Present all year round, they like to visit gardens with birch or alders in winter and will mix with Siskins and Goldfinches. Their irruptive nature makes it hard to know just how many birds are in Britain, but since the 1970s there has been a gradual decline in numbers.

Having a bird-bath in the garden can attract rarer birds, such as Lesser Redpolls. You can encourage them into the garden by planting alders, spruces or birch; they feed on the very small seeds from these trees.

Bullfinch *Pyrrhula pyrrhula*

Occurrence: All year round
Habitats: Orchards, hedgerows, parks and woodland
Garden ranking: RARE

MALE

Pinkish-red cheeks and breast

Grey back

FEMALE

Grey-buff breast with dull pink wash

JUVENILE

Grey-brown all over but still has white rump

White wing-bar

White rump

IDENTIFICATION POINTS
- Big, compact finch
- Black cap
- Pinkish-red cheeks and breast (males)
- White rump in flight

CONFUSION SPECIES AND IDENTIFICATION NOTES
Bright summer males are easy to identify. However, poorly viewed females could be confused with Chaffinches and also with winter Hawfinches, although the latter are larger and far less common.

CHARACTERISTICS

LENGTH: 14.5–16.5 cm

WINGSPAN: 22–29 cm

VOICE: Call is a sad sounding short whistle 'peu'. Song is a slow and tentative mixture of notes, rarely heard.

NESTBOX: No.

NESTING: After male locates a site, the female builds a delicate nest of twigs and roots low to the ground. 4 or 5 purple-streaked, green-blue eggs laid between April–August.

FOOD & FEEDING: Chief food is buds, including oak, hawthorn and fruit trees. Also eats tree flowers, berries and seeds, including dock and bramble. Parents have a pouch in their mouths to help carry food to young. The young eat plant and animal food. Will visit feeders, but cautiously.

Bullfinches can be regular visitors to larger gardens, especially if there is enough cover to hide in. They are fairly shy, preferring to stay hidden in dense cover, and the best way to find them is by learning their call and then waiting for them to fly out. Their white rump is a good aid to identification. They occur across Europe and enjoy a mainly sedentary existence, although birds from north-eastern Europe do migrate, occasionally reaching Britain. These northern birds tend to be slightly larger and brighter in colour.

Bullfinches are very shy. Although they will visit feeders, they usually do so at dawn, when gardens are at their quietest and there is less disturbance.

For years the Bullfinch has had the status of an agricultural pest due to its habit of stripping the buds from fruit trees, damaging potential yields. The loss of hedgerows and weeds in fields means the Bullfinch has to look at other food sources to survive, but overall numbers are falling.

Hawfinch *Coccothraustes coccothraustes*

Occurrence: All year round
Habitats: Mixed and deciduous woodland, especially hornbeam and oak
Garden ranking: RARE

Big head and
thick neck

Massive, conical
blue-black bill (pale
yellow in winter)

Lyre-shaped
tertials

JUVENILE

More orange
on head

Grey-
yellow
breast

Short tail with
white tip

**MALE, SUMMER
PLUMAGE**

Darkly
spotted
belly

Less black
around face

FEMALE

Similar to male, but
generally duller

Grey secondaries
and primaries (not
black as in male)

IDENTIFICATION
POINTS
- Largest finch in UK
- Massive bill
- Looks top-heavy
- Broad, white wing-bar
in flight

CONFUSION SPECIES AND IDENTIFICATION
NOTES
Their large size and stocky appearance separates
them from other finches. Although Chaffinches have
a similar plumage pattern, they are much smaller.
However, Waxwings have a similar stocky build, so
their shape could be confusing.

CHARACTERISTICS

LENGTH: 16.5–18 cm

WINGSPAN: 29–33 cm

VOICE: Call is similar to the Robin's hard 'tic', but is a more abrupt and explosive 'zik'. Song is slow and stumbling, and rarely heard.

NESTBOX: No.

NESTING: Saucer-shaped nest of twigs and moss, usually high in fruit trees. 4–5 blue-green eggs with dark flecks laid between May–July. Both parents feed young.

FOOD & FEEDING: Chief food is tree seeds, such as wild cherry, hornbeam, yew and beech. Also eats hips and haws, buds and some insects in the breeding season. The massive bill is capable of splitting cherry-stones. Has been known to take peas from pods in vegetable gardens.

The Hawfinch is one of our most shy and elusive birds and therefore a real gem to find in your garden. They need mature trees with a variety of seeds and kernels to feed from, and as the average garden doesn't have these, the best places to find them are parks, cemeteries, arboretums and mixed woodland. They prefer to stay well-hidden in the tops of trees, occasionally giving away their presence with their loud 'zik' calls.

Top-heavy appearance

Broad white bands

Short tail

Winter is the best time to see Hawfinches, when the leaves have fallen from the trees and the birds are more exposed to view. Their numbers have dropped recently, possibly due to nest predation by grey squirrels and habitat loss after severe gales in Britain in 1987 toppled thousands of mature trees.

The elusive Hawfinch has been known to visit feeders but it must be one of the rarest garden birds to do so! One of the best ways to see them is when they are feeding from fallen fruit on the ground.

Yellowhammer *Emberiza citrinella*

Occurrence: All year round
Habitats: Open country, farmland and hedgerows
Garden ranking: RARE

MALE, SUMMER PLUMAGE

Brilliant lemon-yellow head

Warm chestnut streaked back

Chestnut rump

Broad, russet breast-band

Long, blackish tail with white outer feathers

FEMALE

Generally much duller than male

Pale yellow wash to face

Chestnut rump

Streaky-brown upperparts

ADULT WINTER

Resembles summer female

Darker cheeks

Duller yellow

IDENTIFICATION POINTS

- Bright-yellow head (summer males)
- Longish, notched tail
- 'Little bit of bread and no cheese' song
- Often sings from hedgerows

CONFUSION SPECIES AND IDENTIFICATION NOTES

The Cirl Bunting looks similar but is rare in the UK and not a regular garden bird. Juvenile Yellow-hammers look similar to Corn Buntings (again, unusual in gardens), but have a smaller bill and a red-brown tone to their plumage.

CHARACTERISTICS

LENGTH: 16–16.5 cm

WINGSPAN: 23–29.5 cm

VOICE: Calls vary: a sharp 'tsit', a drawn out 'tsiih'. Song is the familiar 'little bit of bread and no cheese'.

NESTBOX: No.

NESTING: A bulky platform-nest of grass and straw, low to or on the ground in grass clump or bush. 3–5 pale purplish-white eggs with bold scribbles laid between April–September. Both parents feed young in nest and for a period of time after fledging.

FOOD & FEEDING: Mainly a seed-eater, but also eats insects and spiders, including beetles and caterpillars. Joins mixed finch flocks in winter and will visit gardens, taking spilt seeds from the ground.

A male Yellowhammer in its full, sulphurous-yellow breeding plumage looks more like an exotic escaped cagebird than a UK resident. Sadly, due to a 50 per cent decrease in numbers over the last thirty years, they are now much rarer. Once a familiar part of summer in the countryside, when picnics on hot days were often accompanied by the Yellowhammer's repetitive song, for many this bird is fast becoming a distant memory.

A victim of modern intensive farming methods – which have removed many vital foods – the Yellowhammer has declined alarmingly, along with many other once-widespread farmland birds. Until 'wildlife-friendly' farming is carried out more widely, Yellowhammer numbers are likely to remain depressed, although they are picking up now in some areas.

Juveniles resemble females, but they are generally duller with a streakier head, breast and flanks.

Reed Bunting *Emberiza schoeniclus*

Occurrence: All year round
Habitats: Reedbeds, marshes, hedgerows and farmland
Garden ranking: RARE

MALE, WINTER PLUMAGE

Hint of dark bib

Dark brown head with suggestion of supercilium

MALE, SUMMER PLUMAGE

Jet-black head

Warm chestnut upperparts

White moustachial stripe and collar

Grey-streaked rump

No black head

Dark crown and cheeks

Pale throat and supercilium

FEMALE, SUMMER PLUMAGE

IDENTIFICATION POINTS

- Sparrow-sized bird
- Black head, white collar (males)
- Notched tail
- White or cream moustachial stripe

CONFUSION SPECIES AND IDENTIFICATION NOTES

The adult male is distinctive, but females and juveniles are sometimes confused with female House Sparrows. This usually happens when Reed Buntings are seen feeding away from wetland habitats, such as in gardens! The Little Bunting, a rare migrant to Britain, looks similar to females and juveniles but has warm chestnut cheeks and lacks the supercilium.

160

CHARACTERISTICS

LENGTH: 15–16.5 cm

WINGSPAN: 21–28 cm

VOICE: Calls include a thin 'tseeu' and a ringing 'bzu'. Song is varied, but includes a slow 'hiccoughing' with a faster final flourish.

NESTBOX: No.

NESTING: Female builds a substantial nest of grasses and moss on the ground in a clump of grass or just off the ground in a low bush, usually near water. 4–5 buff eggs with dark streaks laid between April–June. Both parents feed young.

FOOD & FEEDING: Chief food is seeds, mainly from grasses, but also eats insects and invertebrates. Visits gardens in winter to feed from seed-feeders or spilt seed from the ground.

The Reed Bunting is usually associated with reedbeds and other wetland habitats, so it can cause confusion when seen in gardens and on farmland. However, they are increasingly establishing themselves in drier habitats, perhaps due to the loss of suitable wetlands, and are turning up in gardens more often these days.

Sadly, as a farmland bird the Reed Bunting has seen a sharp decrease in its numbers recently. However, its ability to adapt to other habitats may yet help it to survive. Indeed, Reed Buntings can be found anywhere, from young forestry plantations to suburban backyards, so they are always worth looking out for. If recently introduced farming initiatives continue, including an increase in spring seed-sowing, then the Reed Bunting may face a more stable future. Meanwhile, it will continue to benefit from gardens.

During the winter months when seeds from weeds become scarce, watch out for the welcome sight of a Reed Bunting at your feeders.

More Unusual Garden Visitors in Britain and Europe

White Stork *Ciconia ciconia*

Occurrence: Rare visitor to UK, mainly spring/summer. Summer visitor
to Europe, winters in tropical Africa
Habitats: Rooftops, open land, fields, marshes, swampy riversides

ADULT

Red bill

Starkly contrasting
black-and-white
plumage

Soars on slightly
bowed wings

Holds neck
straight out

Legs held
straight out
behind body

Long,
red legs

Deep flaps
when flying

CONFUSION SPECIES AND IDENTIFICATION NOTES
The Grey Heron and possibly the rare Common Crane could cause confusion,
but only in flight. On the ground their stately walk, sheer size and contrasting
markings make them easy to identify.

CHARACTERISTICS
LENGTH: 100–115 cm
WINGSPAN: 175–195 cm
VOICE: Silent, but clatters bill especially when pair together at nest.
NESTBOX: Yes, man-made platform.
NESTING: Huge nest of sticks, usually on roofs, chimneys, telegraph poles etc.
4 white eggs laid between April–July.
FOOD & FEEDING: Almost anything! Small mammals, amphibians, lizards,
insects, birds, carrion.

Ring-necked (Rose-ringed) Parakeet
Psittacula krameri
Occurrence: All year round

Habitats: Parks, gardens, orchards in Southern England and some parts of Europe, especially Netherlands and Belgium

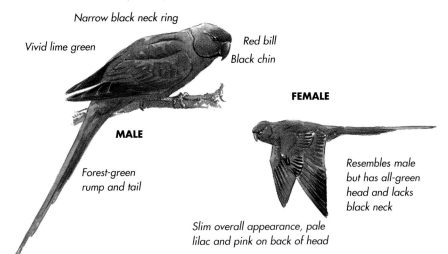

Narrow black neck ring

Vivid lime green

Red bill

Black chin

FEMALE

MALE

Forest-green rump and tail

Resembles male but has all-green head and lacks black neck

Slim overall appearance, pale lilac and pink on back of head

CONFUSION SPECIES AND IDENTIFICATION NOTES
The European Bee-eater could look similar in flight, but nothing other than escapee parakeets should cause real confusion.

CHARACTERISTICS

LENGTH: 38–42 cm

WINGSPAN: 42–48 cm

VOICE: A loud shrill screeching call, often given in flight, but also when perched.

NESTBOX: Yes.

NESTING: Nest is usually an old woodpecker hole in tree, but will also nest in other holes – in buildings or walls for example. 3–4 smooth, non-glossy eggs are laid between January–June. Both parents feed young.

FOOD & FEEDING: A vegetarian diet comprising blossom, fruit, berries, seeds, grain and kitchen scraps. A frequent bird-table visitor, taking peanuts, seeds and chopped fruit.

Hoopoe *Upupa epops*

Occurrence: In Britain from April–June and mid-autumn, occasionally overwintering. Widespread in central and southern Europe
Habitats: During migration they can turn up almost anywhere, otherwise preferring open farmland, pasture and gardens

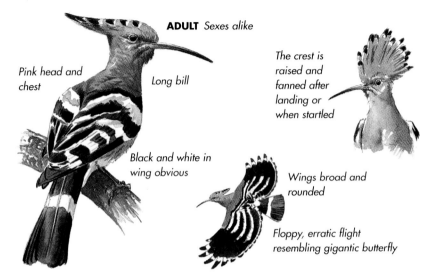

ADULT *Sexes alike*

Pink head and chest

Long bill

The crest is raised and fanned after landing or when startled

Black and white in wing obvious

Wings broad and rounded

Floppy, erratic flight resembling gigantic butterfly

CONFUSION SPECIES AND IDENTIFICATION NOTES

The buff-pink and black-and-white glimpses seen in flight could be confused with the Jay. Nothing else is similar.

CHARACTERISTICS
LENGTH: 26–28 cm
WINGSPAN: 42–46 cm
VOICE: Call is a soft, resonant 'poo-poo-poo'.
NESTBOX: No.
NESTING: In a cavity such as a hole in a tree or building, lined with roots, feathers and wool, and built by both parents. 7–8 non-glossy eggs are laid between April–June. Egg colour varies, greyish, greenish or yellowish. Both parents feed young.
FOOD & FEEDING: Insects such as beetles and crickets, larvae, spiders, slugs, snails and even lizards. Feeds from the ground, either by plucking at food or sticking long bill in the ground to retrieve invertebrates.

Wryneck *Jynx torquilla*

Occurrence: Summer visitor to Europe, April–September. No longer breeds regularly in Britain, but turns up on passage. Winters in tropical Africa
Habitats: Parkland and large mature gardens; also open, scrubby pasture with open woodland, pine and birch woods

Resembles a large bulky warbler in shape

Dark band on back

Amazing cryptic plumage

Yellow-buff throat

ADULT *Sexes alike*

Obvious dark band through eye

CONFUSION SPECIES AND IDENTIFICATION NOTES
The amazing Wryneck looks like nothing else, even though it is classed as a woodpecker. At first it resembles a warbler in shape but it behaves like a thrush on the ground and even like a Treecreeper when clinging to tree trunks.

CHARACTERISTICS
LENGTH: 16–17 cm
WINGSPAN: 25–27 cm
VOICE: Most common call is a ringing, far-carrying, 'quee quee, quee'. Alarm call is a series of hard 'teck' notes. Also makes a hissing noise.
NESTBOX: Yes. Enclosed nestbox.
NESTING: Trees, walls, earthy banks and nestboxes are all used, and Wrynecks have been known to evict other breeding birds. 7-10 white eggs laid between May–August; both parents brood the young.
FOOD & FEEDING: Ants are the Wryneck's chief food, which it uses its long sticky tongue to capture. Other food includes spiders. Chicks are fed ant larvae by both parents.

Nightingale *Luscinia megarhynchos*

Occurrence: A summer visitor to England, April–September
Widespread in Europe. Winters in Africa
Habitats: Scrubby areas, open woodland and woodland edge, dense overgrowth
Can turn up in well-wooded parks and gardens

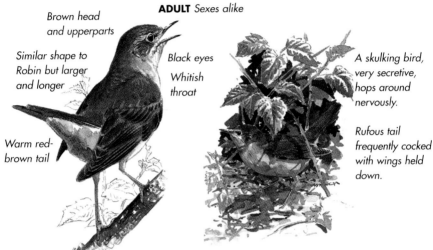

ADULT *Sexes alike*

Brown head
and upperparts

Similar shape to
Robin but larger
and longer

Black eyes

Whitish
throat

Warm red-
brown tail

A skulking bird,
very secretive,
hops around
nervously.

Rufous tail
frequently cocked
with wings held
down.

CONFUSION SPECIES AND IDENTIFICATION NOTES

Robin and Common Redstart, which share similar shape but are smaller.
However, the Nightingale is more secretive and less likely to make itself obvious.

CHARACTERISTICS
LENGTH: 14–16.5 cm
WINGSPAN: 23–26 cm
VOICE: Call is a harsh 'tack, tack' and a grating croak. The beautiful, powerful
and melodic song can be confused with the Song Thrush: a mixture of trills,
fluted whistles and rippling gurgles.
NESTBOX: No.
NESTING: Female builds a nest of leaves, grasses and hair very close to the
ground in dense foliage. 4–5 greyish-brown or olive-coloured eggs laid between
April–July. Both parents feed young.
FOOD & FEEDING: Insects are chief food, including ants and flies, usually eaten
from the ground in dense cover. Also eats berries in autumn.

Black Redstart *Phoenicurus ochruros*

Occurrence: All year round in some parts of Britain, with small breeding population;
more in autumn due to migrants. Widespread in Europe

Habitats: Can turn up almost anywhere, from cities to upland slopes and rocky
coastal shores, especially on migration

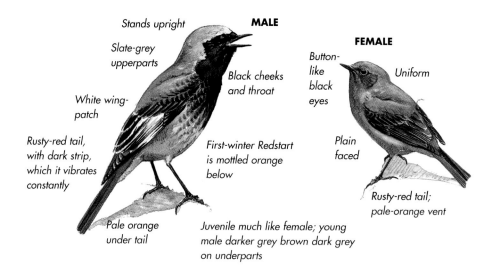

Stands upright

MALE

Slate-grey
upperparts

Black cheeks
and throat

White wing-
patch

Rusty-red tail,
with dark strip,
which it vibrates
constantly

First-winter Redstart
is mottled orange
below

Pale orange
under tail

Juvenile much like female; young
male darker grey brown dark grey
on underparts

FEMALE

Button-
like
black
eyes

Uniform

Plain
faced

Rusty-red tail;
pale-orange vent

CONFUSION SPECIES AND IDENTIFICATION NOTES

Even though the Common Redstart has an orange breast and underparts, at a
distance its shape and behaviour can be confusing.

CHARACTERISTICS

LENGTH: 13.5–14.5 cm

WINGSPAN: 23–26 cm

VOICE: Call is a loud whistling 'vist'. Song is a series of fast whistles and rattles,
like metal balls shaken in a bag.

NESTBOX: Yes.

NESTING: Similar to Common Redstart (but not in tree holes). Female builds nest of
mosses, dead grass and bark bits, lined with hair and feathers. 4–6 white eggs laid
between April–July. Male helps to feed chicks.

FOOD & FEEDING: As for Common Redstart.

Common Redstart
Phoenicurus phoenicurus

Occurrence: A fairly common summer visitor to parts of the UK, with regular migrants in spring and autumn. Widespread in Europe

Habitats: Deciduous woodland, parks, gardens and heaths with trees

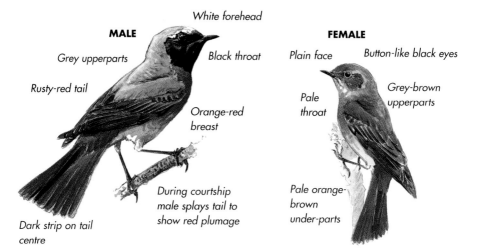

White forehead

MALE

Grey upperparts

Black throat

Rusty-red tail

Orange-red breast

During courtship male splays tail to show red plumage

Dark strip on tail centre

FEMALE

Plain face

Button-like black eyes

Pale throat

Grey-brown upperparts

Pale orange-brown under-parts

CONFUSION SPECIES AND IDENTIFICATION NOTES

Black Redstarts, Robins and Nightingales could be confused. Redstarts and Robins share similar behaviour; legs always darker on Common and Black Redstarts.

CHARACTERISTICS

LENGTH: 13–14 cm

WINGSPAN: 20.5–24 cm

VOICE: Call is a whistled 'huitt-ticc-ticc'; song a brief, melancholic high-pitched warble, ending in a mechanical rattle.

NESTBOX: Yes

NESTING: In holes and crevices, especially in dry-stone walls and trees. Female builds nest of mosses, dead grass and bark bits, lined with hair and feathers. 5–7 pale blue eggs laid between April–June. Male helps to feed chicks.

FOOD & FEEDING: Chief food is insects, especially flies and beetles. Also eats spiders, worms, seeds and berries.

Whitethroat *Sylvia communis*

Occurrence: A common regular visitor to UK (May–August) and Europe; winters in Africa, south of the Sahara

Habitats: Open areas and woodland edge, with hedgerows, brambles and nettles

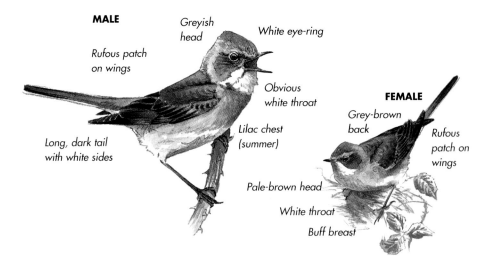

MALE — Greyish head — White eye-ring — Rufous patch on wings — Obvious white throat — **FEMALE** — Grey-brown back — Rufous patch on wings — Long, dark tail with white sides — Lilac chest (summer) — Pale-brown head — White throat — Buff breast

CONFUSION SPECIES AND IDENTIFICATION NOTES

The Lesser Whitethroat looks similar, but appears more grey than brown on upperparts and is more skulking.

CHARACTERISTICS

LENGTH: 13–14 cm

WINGSPAN: 18.5–23 cm

VOICE: Has a mixture of calls, from a nasal 'ved, ved, ved', usually when alarmed, to a drawn-out 'chaihr' and a hard 'tac, tac' Song is a fast and blustery, scratchy warble.

NESTBOX: No.

NESTING: Male builds several incomplete 'cock nests' for female to choose one. The cup-shaped nest is usually low down in amongst dense foliage, especially nettles. 4–5 pale eggs with dark spots are laid between April–July.

FOOD & FEEDING: Mainly insects in the breeding season, especially flies and caterpillars. Eats berries towards end of summer in preparation for migration.

Firecrest *Regulus ingicapillus*

Occurrence: All year round in some parts of England, but mainly on migration in spring and autumn. More widespread in Europe in winter.
Habitats: Woodland, especially spruce plantations but also deciduous. Also scrub, gardens and coastal habitats on passage

MALE

Orange-coloured central stripe to crown

Broad white supercilium

Dark eye-stripe

FEMALE

Yellow central crown stripe

Dark eye-stripe

Bronze neck patch

Bronze patch

Pale-grey underparts

Broad white supercilium

No colour on crown

Pale supercilium

JUVENILE

CONFUSION SPECIES AND IDENTIFICATION NOTES

Goldcrest looks and behaves similarly, but lacks the broad white supercilium. Firecrests also have a black eye-stripe plus a bronze-coloured patch on sides of neck. The very rare autumn-visiting Pallas's Warbler also looks similar.

CHARACTERISTICS

LENGTH: 9–10 cm
WINGSPAN: 13–16 cm
VOICE: Call is a strident 'zi-zi-zi', lower-pitched than Goldcrest. Song is a thin, simple repetition of one note.
NESTBOX: No.
NESTING: Ball-shaped nest of moss and spiders' webs suspended from branch, made by female. 7–11 white or pinkish eggs speckled brown, May–June.
FOOD & FEEDING: Insects, spiders, aphids, flies and caterpillars. Spends most of its day flicking through leaves searching for food. A very unlikely visitor to the bird-table, although harsh weather occasionally forces them to take tit-bits.

Pied Flycatcher *Ficedula hypoleuca*

Occurrence: Summer visitor and local breeder in western Britain; more widespread on migration. Common in Europe, winters in West Africa
Habitats: Parks, gardens and deciduous open forest; sometimes in pinewoods

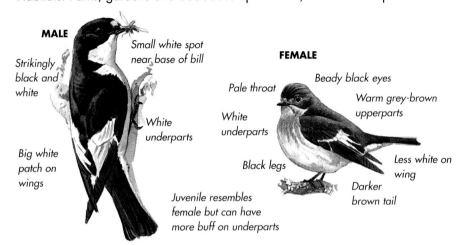

MALE

Strikingly black and white

Small white spot near base of bill

White underparts

Big white patch on wings

FEMALE

Pale throat

White underparts

Black legs

Beady black eyes

Warm grey-brown upperparts

Less white on wing

Darker brown tail

Juvenile resembles female but can have more buff on underparts

CONFUSION SPECIES AND IDENTIFICATION NOTES
Spotted Flycatcher looks similar to female or young, but is more streaked on the breast and has no white wing panel.

CHARACTERISTICS
LENGTH: 12–13 cm
WINGSPAN: 21.5–24 cm
VOICE: Calls are a sharp 'pwit' and quiet clicking 'tec'. Song is a loud, ringing but slightly melancholic 'tsuee-tsuee-tsuee weecha weecha chuvee chuvee'.
NESTBOX: Yes. Enclosed nestbox.
NESTING: Female builds a loose nest of grasses, moss and roots in a hole in a tree, often an old woodpecker nest. 4–7 unmarked pale-blue eggs laid between April–June. Both parents feed young. Males are bigamous, but less likely to feed second or even third broods.
FOOD & FEEDING: Mainly insects, but also some fruits and seeds. Will eat worms and even small snails, hammering them out like a Song Thrush. Catches food in the air, but also from leaves or the ground. A rare visitor to the bird-table, but nestboxes in wooded gardens may encourage them to breed.

Serin *Serinus serinus*

Occurrence: A rare spring/summer visitor to England, and occasionally breeds, mainly in the south. More common and widespread in Europe
Habitats: Parks and gardens, and in Europe olive groves, churchyards and Mediterranean woodland.

MALE
Tiny, stubby bill
Small, chunky-looking finch
Heavy streaking on back
Yellow rump
Two narrow wing-bars

Darker cheeks
Less yellow on face
Darker, streakier version of male
FEMALE

CONFUSION SPECIES AND IDENTIFICATION NOTES
The Siskin, Greenfinch and Yellowhammer are most likely to cause confusion, not forgetting the occasional escaped Canary! The Serin's heavy streaks are obvious.

CHARACTERISTICS
LENGTH: 11–12 cm
WINGSPAN: 20–23 cm
VOICE: Call, often in flight, is a jingling, high-pitched 'tirillillit'; also a Greenfinch-like 'juwee'. Song is a prolonged, very fast chirping, jingling notes.
NESTBOX: No.
NESTING: Female builds a delicate, well-hidden nest of grasses, lichens, moss and tiny roots, bound with spiders' webs. 3–5 eggs laid between April–August. Both parents feed the young; male becomes sole feeder if female nests again.
FOOD & FEEDING: Eats mainly seeds from weeds, but also insects, especially in the breeding season. Will take tree buds, such as birch and beech.

Useful Addresses and Further Reading

USEFUL ADDRESSES

BTO (British Trust for Ornithology)
The Nunnery
Thetford
Norfolk
IP24 2PU
Tel: 01842 750050
www.bto.org
www.bto.org/gbw (for information about Garden BirdWatch)
www.bto.org/birdfacts (a one-stop-shop for answers to commonly asked questions)
www.bto.org/birdtrends (trends in numbers and breeding performance in UK birds)

Founded in 1933, the BTO carries out research into the lives of birds by conducting population and breeding surveys, and bird ringing, through the activities of its 30,000 volunteers. The Trust publishes a bimonthly members' magazine called *BTO News*.

RSPB (Royal Society for the Protection of Birds)
The Lodge
Sandy
Bedfordshire
SG19 2DL
Tel: 01767 680551
www.rspb.org.uk

The RSPB was set up in 1889 and is now Europe's largest wildlife conservation charity, with over one million members. It publishes a quarterly members' magazine called *BIRDS*.

BSA (Birdcare Standards Association)
PO Box 361
Cleethorpes
DN35 7XQ
www.birdcare.org.uk

A not-for-profit association of the UK's leading suppliers of wild-bird care products. The aim is to promote best practice by ensuring that only safe and nutritious products are provided to wild bird populations.

Gardman Ltd
High Street
Moulton
Spalding
Lincs
PE12 6QD
Tel: 01406 372237
www.gardman.co.uk

Gardman is the UK's brand leader in the wild-bird care category, offering over 230 different products. Most Gardman products are tested and endorsed by the BTO and meet all the BSA (Bird Care Standards Association) standards. Gardman also provides the BTO with its own branded range of bird foods.

CJ Wildbird Foods Ltd
The Rea
Upton Magna
Shrewsbury
SY4 4UB
Tel: 01743 709545
www.birdfood.co.uk

CJ Wildbird Foods is one of the leading suppliers of mail order bird feeders, nestboxes and foodstuffs. The company sponsors the BTO's Garden BirdWatch survey.

Jacobi Jayne Ltd
Freepost 1155
Herne Bay
Kent
CT6 7BR
Tel: 01227-714311
www.jacobijayne.co.uk

Founding sponsor of National Nestbox Week, organized by the BTO, Jacobi Jayne offers a wide range of high quality bird care products.

FURTHER READING

Books

Bill Oddie's Introduction to Birdwatching
Bill Oddie
New Holland
ISBN 1 85974 894 5

The BTO Nestbox Guide
Chris du Feu
BTO Publications
ISBN 1 902576 81 0

The Birdwatcher's Garden
Hazel Johnson & Pamela Johnson
Guild of Master Craftman Publications
ISBN 1 86108 135 9

Garden Bird Behaviour
Robert Burton
New Holland
ISBN 1 84330 938 6

The Garden Bird Year
Roy Beddard
New Holland
ISBN 1 85974 951 8

The BTO/CJ Garden BirdWatch Handbook
Mike Toms
BTO Publications
ISBN 1 902576 73 X

The State of the Nations' Birds
Chris Mead
Whittet Books
ISBN 1873580 45 2

Time to Fly
Jim Flegg
BTO Publications
ISBN 1 904870 08 2

The Ultimate Birdfeeder Handbook
John A.Burton & Steve Young
New Holland
ISBN 1 84330 956 4

Magazines

BBC Wildlife
Available monthly from most news-agents, or by subscription from:
BBC Wildlife Subscriptions, PO Box 425, Woking, Surrey, GU21 1GP

Bird Watching
Available monthly from most news-agents, or by subscription from:
Bird Watching subscriptions, Tower House, Sovereign Park, Market Harborough, Leicester, LE16 9EF

Birdwatch
Available monthly by subscription from:
Birdwatch, Solo Publications Ltd, The Chocolate Factory, 5 Clarendon Road, London N22 6XJ

British Birds
Available monthly by subscription from:
Hazel Jenner at subscriptions@helm-information.co.uk

Index